The Shakespeare Handbooks: Shakespeare's Contemporaries
Series Editors: Paul Edmondson & Kevin Ewert

The White Devil is one of the great plays of the Jacobean era. In this vibrant Handbook, Stephen Purcell offers an in-depth, performance-focused exploration of John Webster's thrilling, unsettling and darkly comic tragedy. The Handbook includes:

- a scene-by-scene commentary on the play as it unfolds on stage
- an overview of the play's cultural context
- excerpts from historical sources
- case studies of four modern productions, featuring interviews with directors
- an outline of key critical writings on the play, from the seventeenth century through to today.

Stephen Purcell is Assistant Professor of English at The University of Warwick. His previous publications include *Popular Shakespeare* (2009) and he is Artistic Director of The Pantaloons, an open-air theatre company.

The Shakespeare Handbooks are student-friendly introductory guides which offer a new approach to understanding the plays of Shakespeare and his contemporaries in performance. The commentary at the heart of each volume explores the play's theatrical potential, providing an experience as close as possible to seeing it in the theatre. Ideal for students and teachers of Literature and Theatre, as well as actors and directors, the overall aim is to help a reader reach an independent and well-informed view of each play by imagining how it might be rehearsed or performed on stage.

THE SHAKESPEARE HANDBOOKS

Series Editors: Paul Edmondson and Kevin Ewert
(Founding Series Editor: John Russell Brown)

PUBLISHED

John Russell Brown	*Hamlet*
John Russell Brown	*Macbeth*
John Russell Brown	*King Lear*
David Carnegie	*Julius Caesar*
Paul Edmondson	*Twelfth Night*
Bridget Escolme	*Antony and Cleopatra*
Kevin Ewert	*Henry V*
Alison Findlay	*Much Ado about Nothing*
Trevor R. Griffiths	*The Tempest*
Stuart Hampton-Reeves	*Measure for Measure*
Stuart Hampton-Reeves	*Othello*
Margaret Jane Kidnie	*The Taming of the Shrew*
Ros King	*The Winter's Tale*
James N. Loehlin	*Henry IV, Parts I and II*
Jeremy Lopez	*Richard II*
Edward L. Rocklin	*Romeo and Juliet*
Lesley Wade Soule	*As You Like It*
Martin White	*A Midsummer Night's Dream*

SHAKESPEARE'S CONTEMPORARIES

Jay O'Berski	Middleton and Rowley: *The Changeling*
Stephen Purcell	Webster: *The White Devil*
Martin White	Ford: *'Tis Pity She's a Whore*

Other titles are currently in preparation

The Shakespeare Handbooks:
Shakespeare's Contemporaries

John Webster
The White Devil

Stephen Purcell

First published 2012 by
PALGRAVE MACMILLAN

Palgrave Macmillan in the UK is an imprint of Macmillan Publishers Limited, registered in England, company number 785998, of Houndmills, Basingstoke, Hampshire RG21 6XS.

Palgrave Macmillan in the US is a division of St Martin's Press LLC, 175 Fifth Avenue, New York, NY 10010.

Palgrave Macmillan is the global academic imprint of the above companies and has companies and representatives throughout the world.

Palgrave® and Macmillan® are registered trademarks in the United States, the United Kingdom, Europe and other countries.

ISBN-13: 978–0–230–27975–9 hardback
ISBN-13: 978–0–230–27976–6 paperback

This book is printed on paper suitable for recycling and made from fully managed and sustained forest sources. Logging, pulping and manufacturing processes are expected to conform to the environmental regulations of the country of origin.

A catalogue record for this book is available from the British Library.

A catalog record for this book is available from the Library of Congress.

10 9 8 7 6 5 4 3 2 1
21 20 19 18 17 16 15 14 13 12

Printed in China

For Zoë

Contents

Series Editors' Preface

The Shakespeare Handbooks provide an innovative way of studying the plays of Shakespeare and his contemporaries in performance. The commentaries, which are their core feature, enable a reader to envisage the words of a text unfurling in performance, involving actions and meanings not readily perceived except in rehearsal or performance. The aim is to present the plays in the environment for which they were written and to offer an experience as close as possible to an audience's progressive experience of a production.

While each book has the same range of contents, their authors have been encouraged to shape them according to their own critical and scholarly understanding and their first-hand experience of theatre practice. The various chapters are designed to complement the commentaries: the cultural context of each play is presented together with quotations from original sources; the authority of its text or texts is considered with what is known of the earliest performances; key performances and productions of its subsequent stage history are both described and compared; an account is given of influential criticism of the play and the more significant is quoted extensively. The aim in all this has been to help readers to develop their own informed and imaginative view of a play in ways that supplement the provision of standard editions and are more user-friendly than detailed stage histories or collections of criticism from diverse sources.

We would like to acknowledge a special debt of gratitude to the founder of the Shakespeare Handbooks Series, John Russell Brown, whose energy for life, literature and theatre we continue to find truly inspiring.

Paul Edmondson and Kevin Ewert

Preface

Like all great plays, *The White Devil* is both a work of literature and a blueprint for theatrical performance. The experience of reading it can be immeasurably rewarding, but the experience of watching it in the theatre will more often than not draw attention to its potential as a thrilling, dynamic, surprising, thought-provoking and unsettling piece of performance. This handbook is designed to assist the reader in thinking through the play's theatrical possibilities, whether as groundwork for an actual production of the play, or as the basis for an imagined one. Chapters 1 and 3 give a sense of its original context, allowing the reader to imagine some of the ways in which the play might have worked for its original audiences. Chapter 2, by far the longest section of the book, is a scene-by-scene commentary which explores the theatrical workings in detail. Chapter 4 looks at the choices made in specific productions, organizing its analysis around a series of key topics, while Chapter 5 examines some of the various ways in which the text has been interpreted by literary critics over the centuries. I have been keen to emphasize that there is no 'right' way to stage *The White Devil*; rather, I hope that this book will aid readers in formulating, exploring and researching their own interpretations of the text. Readers familiar with the Handbooks series will note the absence of a chapter on screen versions of the play: this is because there have been, to date, no television or film adaptations of *The White Devil*.

All citations from *The White Devil* are from John Russell Brown's 1996 Revels Student edition. Citations from *The Jew of Malta*, *The Revenger's Tragedy*, *The Duchess of Malfi* and *'Tis Pity She's a Whore* are from David Bevington's *English Renaissance Drama: A Norton Anthology* (2002), and all citations from Shakespeare are from Stanley Wells and Gary Taylor's *Complete Works* (Oxford, 1986). Newspaper articles are not listed in the bibliography: where cited, newspaper and date of publication are listed in the main body of the text. Spellings have been standardized to British, and spellings in sources written before 1800 have been modernized.

Thanks are due to Paul Edmondson, John Russell Brown and all at Palgrave Macmillan for their guidance and support during the book's preparation. The directors Philip Franks and Jonathan Munby both very generously gave up their time to record interviews for Chapter 4, for which I am extremely grateful. Thanks to Andy Kesson, Farah Karim-Cooper and The Pantaloons theatre company, I was able to explore excerpts from *The White Devil* with a team of highly imaginative actors on the stage of Shakespeare's Globe, which was immeasurably useful. The staff of the National Theatre Archive and the Shakespeare Birthplace Trust were also very helpful in providing me with access to invaluable archive material.

Every effort has been made to trace rights holders but if any have been inadvertently overlooked, the Publishers will be pleased to make the necessary arrangement at the first opportunity.

1 The Text and First Performances

The White Devil was first performed in early 1612, and published shortly afterwards. Its first performances were at the open-air Red Bull playhouse, where it was not particularly well-received: Webster's own preface to the play notes that it was 'acted in so dull a time of winter, presented in so open and black a theatre, that it wanted...a full and understanding auditory'. The Red Bull had a reputation for being 'mostly frequented by citizens, and the meaner sort of people' (James Wright, *Historia Histrionica*, 1699), and its audience was often characterized as being uncomprehending: Thomas Tomkis's 1615 play *Albumazar*, for example, depicts a rustic clown who regularly frequents the Red Bull, 'where I learn all the words I speak and understand not' (Gurr 2004: 301, 274). Indeed, Webster described his Red Bull audience as 'ignorant asses' and 'uncapable', and in 1617, his writing was satirized by Henry Fitzjeffrey for being 'so obscure, / That none shall understand him'. Webster was, at least, satisfied with the actors' performances, which he commends in the play's Epilogue – drawing particular attention to the 'well approved industry' of the actor Richard Perkins, who probably played Flamineo.

It is important to remember the layout of the theatre and the conditions of staging when reading the play. Webster himself described the experience of theatregoing in his 'Character of an Excellent Actor' in 1615: 'Sit in a full theatre, and you will think you see so many lines drawn from the circumference of so many ears, whiles the actor is the centre.' *The White Devil* would have been performed upon a stage which jutted out into a probably very rowdy audience of standing playgoers, surrounded on at least three sides (if not four) by audience members seated in raised galleries. Soliloquies would thus have been dynamic interactions with a live audience, and scenes like the trial

(III.ii) must have involved some very real public display and crowd-stirring rhetoric. Though the play is set in sixteenth-century Italy, there must have been a sense in its original performances that it was also grounded in the here-and-now of Jacobean London; indeed, Webster makes several anachronistic references to such specifically English subjects as the showman 'Wolner of England' (III.iii.51), the nearby Bishopsgate 'Artillery Yard' (V.vi.160) and even the Tower of London (V.vi.266). Interestingly, it is nearly always Flamineo who makes these local and topical references, which implies that Webster allows him a significantly closer relationship with the audience than he does the other characters.

The printed play's title page describes it as 'The Tragedy of Paulo Giordano Orsini, Duke of Brachiano, with The Life and Death of Vittoria Corombona the famous Venetian Curtizan'. The play was based on the true story of Vittoria Accoramboni, who had been murdered 27 years previously in Padua, Italy, and she is probably the 'white devil' of the title: the phrase was understood at the time as referring to a seemingly innocent person who is in fact guilty, and Vittoria is the only one of the two characters referred to on the title page who fits this description (Bracciano's guilt is fairly evident). She is also the character who is likened by the other characters to a 'devil' most frequently throughout the play. A sermon by the clergyman Thomas Adams, also written in 1612, hints at a possible alternative meaning, however. Titled 'The White Devil, or, The Hypocrite Uncased', Adams's sermon focuses on Christ's betrayer Judas, whom he describes as 'a devil ... black within and full of rancour, but white without, and skinned over with hypocrisy' (1612: 221). 'Of all earthly creatures', he continues,

> a wicked man is the worst, of all men a wicked Christian, of all Christians a wicked professor, of all professors a wicked hypocrite, of all hypocrites a wicked, warped, wretched Judas. Take the extraction or quintessence of all corrupted men, and you have a Judas. This then is a Judas: a man degenerate, a Christian corrupted, a professor putrefied, a gilded hypocrite, a white-skinned devil. (1612: 234)

Of all the characters in Webster's play, the description is perhaps most applicable to Monticelso, a corrupted Christian who, in his role as Pope, would have been encased in white.

The first edition of the text was printed in 1612 by Nicholas Okes, and was probably supervised by Webster himself. Modern editions of the play are largely faithful to this, though most modernize the spelling, add punctuation, and insert act and scene divisions (the scenes are not numbered in the first Quarto). A notable feature of the original text is the large number of non-speaking characters: four are named (Little Jaques the Moor, Christophero, Guid-Antonio and Fernese), though they are never referenced directly in the dialogue itself, while many more are unnamed servants and attendants of various sorts. Martin Wiggins suggests that 'the crowdedness of the play works to enhance our sense of the urban society in which it is set', and argues that 'the spectacular scenes help to define by contrast the quietness and simplicity of others with which they are juxtaposed' (1997: 459, 461). Flamineo's 'final descent down the greasy pole of power', for example, is emphasized in Act V by the number of courtiers who have been advanced ahead of him (1997: 460).

The play was reprinted three times over the century following its first publication, in 1631, in 1665 and in 1672. Each of these editions testifies to the play's continued performance: the 1631 text records performances by Queen Henrietta's company at the Phoenix, Drury Lane, while the 1665 text states that the play was being acted 'at this present (by His now Majesties) at the Theatre Royal'. The 1672 edition confirms that it was still in performance by the King's Company at Bridges Street. Samuel Pepys saw a performance of *The White Devil* in October 1661, describing it as 'a very poor play' and complaining that 'I never had so little pleasure in a play in my life'. Oddly, this did not prevent him from returning to the production two days later, when it pleased him 'worse than it did the other day' (ii, 114, 116). The following century, Nahum Tate (who famously adapted *King Lear* to give it a happy ending) published a 'much simplified and sentimentalized version' of *The White Devil* in 1707 (Holdsworth 1984: 14). In this adaptation, titled *Injur'd Love: or, The Cruel Husband*, Isabella became a much more central character, Bracciano an unambiguous villain and Vittoria innocent. It was, according to its title page, 'designed to be acted at the Theatre Royal', but it was probably never performed. There are no further recorded performances of the play until the twentieth century.

2   *Commentary: the Play in Performance*

This chapter of the book offers a scene-by-scene, moment-by-moment commentary on the play as it might work in performance. Sometimes it explores the perspective of an audience seeing it for the first time, considering the play's surprises, release of information and creation of tension. It frequently examines the play's scope for choices by actors and directors, and weighs up potential staging or interpretative problems. It traces the development and interplay of the play's themes. Elsewhere, it draws attention to some of the ways in which the play might have worked for its original audience. The commentary is designed to be read alongside the play itself, and is based on the Revels Student edition of the text (1996), edited by John Russell Brown.

Act I

Act I, scene i

The play opens *in medias res*, or 'in the middle of things' – the audience are required to work out where the scene is set and who its characters are, as they listen to a conversation about something that has evidently only just happened. To an audience new to the play, Lodovico may at first appear to be its protagonist, and although he takes a much less prominent role later on, he dominates its first scene. This scene also sets up some of the key thematic concerns of the play: in particular, the corruption and inequalities of the law, characters' loss of control over their own destinies and, through Lodovico's opening image of Fortune as a 'whore' (l. 4), the mistrust of female sexuality. The overcharged emotion and the very high number of shared lines imply that this short scene is probably played at a fast pace.

1 Lodovico responds to the news of his banishment. It may be that all three characters enter together mid-conversation, having heard the sentence offstage; alternatively, Antonelli and Gasparo may present Lodovico with a written decree. Either way, this opening constructs the stage as an unofficial space on the periphery of the court, and sets the tone for much of what will follow: this play will focus on the actions of figures lurking in the shadows of official political culture.

2–12 Lodovico is bitter and sarcastic. This important exchange states the twin factors which motivate many of the characters' actions throughout the play: 'Courtly reward, / And punishment' (ll. 3–4). Lodovico curses the goddess Fortuna, the turning of whose wheel was thought, in classical philosophy, to bring about reversals in mortals' luck. His description of her as a 'whore' is the first of many examples of misogynistic language (l. 4). Images of wolves and destructive thunder will also recur at important moments (see, for example, the moments when specific characters are likened to wolves at III.ii.180, IV.ii.91–2, V.i.154–5, and V.iv.35–6, and the moments in which thunder is used as a metaphor for violent destruction at II.i.63–73, III.iii.128, IV.i.22, and V.vi.276). In blaming his misfortune on 'great enemies' rather than his own actions, Lodovico evokes a world in which morality is secondary to power (l. 7).

12–30 Antonelli and Gasparo speak almost as one voice, completing one another's sentences (indeed, some productions combine these roles into a single speaker). They link Lodovico's self-destructive violence with potent images of disease and death (mummia was made from mummified flesh). Lodovico's observation that they are like two buckets coming up and down from a well suggests one way in which this exchange might be staged, as well as mocking their observations as mechanical.

30–3 We learn the reasons for Lodovico's banishment: he has committed several murders which Gasparo describes as 'Bloody and full of horror' (l. 32). Lodovico's perspective, however, is entirely different: to him, the crimes were 'flea-bitings' (l. 32). Such an amoral view of murder, and the refusal to recognize its human consequences, recurs throughout the play in a variety of different characters.

34–53 Gasparo and Antonelli's speeches here are full of *sententiae*: moral observations, often metaphorical, and frequently in the form of rhyming couplets. Their full lines and careful rhymes contrast with Lodovico's much less patterned, more aggressive and unpredictable speech. The idea that 'affliction / Expresseth virtue' (ll. 49–50) was a convention of classical tragedy: though suffering, the hero would achieve ennoblement (see 'Jacobean tragedy', Chapter 3). Does the play prove Antonelli correct? Lodovico responds by suggesting that his friends' *sententiae* are 'painted comforts' – superficial and false – and promises violent reprisal for his enemies (ll. 51–3).

38–44 These few lines introduce the play's protagonists. Webster's audience would probably have recognized these names, having heard the scandalous story of the characters' real-life counterparts (see 'Webster's sources' and 'The Murder of the Signora Accaramboni', Chapter 3). Lodovico's complaint that Vittoria failed to solicit a pardon for him from the Duke suggests a motivation for his actions later in the play, but his expectation that it *might* have happened further implies a world riddled with political corruption. Lodovico's reasons for expecting that Vittoria should have spoken up in his defence are not made clear, and are up to the actor to decide.

53–8 Line 53 is split between three speeches, emphasizing the violence of the exchange. Lodovico's sarcasm becomes apparent once again: but is he referring to his enemies or to his friends as the 'hangmen' with whom he has 'grown familiar' (ll. 55–6)? The force of this passage may be stronger if Antonelli and Gasparo were indeed implicated in handing Lodovico his sentence at start of the scene.

58–63 Antonelli promises to attempt to persuade those in power to repeal Lodovico's banishment. Lines 55 and 61 could be read as indications that Lodovico gives him some money to aid him in this purpose, though the second of these may be referring simply to Lodovico's cynical closing couplet.

60 s.d.   The scene is brought to an abrupt close by a 'sennet' – a trumpet fanfare accompanying a ceremonial entrance. We know that this scene has taken place on the periphery of power, a halfway-space between the political centre of Rome and the space to which Lodovico will be banished; perhaps the characters now flee as the stage is about to be filled with representatives of authority. The moment represents the sudden intrusion of official power into a scene, and play, which has heretofore been concerned only with the unofficial and the marginal.

Act I, scene ii

Having introduced some of the play's central themes, Webster now plunges straight into the plot. This scene is long and dynamic, introducing the three main characters and depicting the events which will provoke the rest of the action. It begins as comedy, moves into intrigue, and then culminates in full-scale confrontation. The scene's alternation of images of luxury with images of decay sets an uncomfortable tone which links the pleasures of the flesh with connotations of hell.

Particularly striking in this scene is the extent to which Flamineo (Vittoria's brother and Bracciano's secretary) commands the stage. Vittoria and Bracciano are, nominally at least, the central characters; the play's original title page billed it as 'The Tragedy of Paolo Giordano Orsini, Duke of Brachiano, With The Life and Death of Vittoria Corombona the famous Venetian Curtizan'. Here, however, Bracciano seems merely to respond to events rather than to instigate them, while Vittoria remains curiously unavailable to the audience, speaking very little until the second half of the scene. Flamineo, on the other hand, is onstage throughout, speaks at length, drives the action, and strikes up a rapport with the audience which will last until the final scene.

1–2   This economical opening establishes a great deal in just two lines. Bracciano's words indicate that it is night-time, while Vittoria's response makes it clear to the audience that he is a Duke, that he is her guest, and that she is also of an elevated social status. The arrangement of bodies on the stage is likely to show, furthermore, that she and Camillo are husband and wife, and that the Duke is well attended. Having heard about 'The Duke of Bracciano' in the previous scene, the audience are likely to identify this Duke immediately as that very man. They know already that he 'seeks to prostitute / The honour of Vittoria Corombona' (I.i.41–2), and indeed it rapidly becomes apparent that the female character onstage is also that woman.

Camillo and Vittoria depart the scene almost straight away, but not before some further hints at the likely success of Bracciano's designs: Vittoria's completion of his half-line of iambic pentameter and her echoing of his word 'best' imply some level of sympathy between the two. It is significant that it is she, not Camillo, who bids the Duke good night. Flamineo tells Bracciano that Vittoria was unable to take her eyes off him (l. 12): it may be that the audience see some evidence of this attraction as she leaves the stage.

3–9 The first exchange between Bracciano and Flamineo establishes an urgent tone and suggests the complicity between them: a single line of iambic pentameter is split between them three ways (l. 3). Note that Bracciano presents his situation as 'quite lost': the scene will go on to show him to be both out of control and morally 'lost', and indeed he will repeat the word towards the end (l. 208). There may also be an echo of Lodovico, who opened the previous scene by declaring himself 'banished'. Flamineo's whispered promise confirms Vittoria's identity to the audience, and introduces an element of secrecy to the scene.

10–16 With the departure of the attendants and their torches, the stage suddenly empties and darkens: clearly the conversation between Flamineo and Bracciano is not one which should be overheard. Flamineo tells us that he has 'dealt already' with Vittoria's chambermaid Zanche (l. 13); much later in the play, we will learn that Flamineo and Zanche have had a sexual relationship. The actor playing Flamineo might hint at this later development in his delivery of these lines.

17–25 With nobody left onstage to overhear them, Flamineo assures his employer that 'We may now talk freely' (l. 17). It is significant that both characters here abandon the formality of verse for casual prose. Webster's audience would have recognized verse as the heightened language spoken by tragic figures of elevated social status, while this sort of prose would have been closer to the 'unofficial' language of ordinary people (including the audience themselves). Flamineo is dropping the outward appearance of nobility and aligning himself with the audience.

His cynicism and misogyny in this passage would also have identified him to the Jacobean audience as a recognizable dramatic type: the malcontent (see 'Jacobean tragedy', Chapter 3). Like many of Shakespeare's malcontents – Iago in *Othello*, Edmund in *King Lear*, Richard III – Flamineo is a bitter, sarcastic outsider, who acts only for his own advancement and takes a perverse enjoyment in manipulating his unsuspecting victims. Like Shakespeare's malcontents, too, he is the figure in the play who speaks most frequently to the audience, fostering a kind of collusion with them. As with many such characters, there may be, for the audience, a morally ambiguous pleasure in watching this skilled and cynical manipulator at work.

26–34   Flamineo's overblown slights to the absent Camillo's manliness and sexual prowess are likely to make an audience laugh: does this increase the audience's complicity in his actions?

35–47   Flamineo, not Bracciano, drives the action here. A social inferior taking charge of his master's love affairs and helping him to cuckold a jealous fool was a stock scenario in comedies of the period, and Flamineo's hasty dispatching of Bracciano into a 'closet' serves to reinforce the comic tone.

His jaded description of an unsuccessful courtship introduces a rather unsettling metaphor: that of a 'summer bird-cage in a garden' (ll. 43–4). The idea that all the characters in the play are struggling either to break into a world from which they feel excluded, or out from a world in which they feel trapped, is an important one. Flamineo will return to the bird-cage metaphor at the end of the play (see V.iv.124).

48–51   Jealous, foolish and easily manipulated, Camillo is another recognizable character type: the comic cuckold. Whether he remains a comic figure or is capable of soliciting more sympathy from an audience will vary from production to production. The extent to which Camillo is played sympathetically will have a direct, inverse effect upon the audience's level of sympathy for his unfaithful wife Vittoria.

Flamineo's aside to the audience (the first aside of the play so far) further establishes him as the audience's primary point of contact in the world of the play.

51–75 The scene moves back into verse, but the tone remains lowbrow. This exchange is full of innuendo, to which Camillo is oblivious; the audience are likely to laugh at him, sharing Flamineo's cruel enjoyment of Camillo's implied sexual inadequacies. Following Camillo's admission that he cannot remember the last time he slept with his wife, Flamineo's reply ('Strange that you should so lose your count', l. 57) is an obscene pun. His quibbling on the word 'flaw' is similarly bawdy, and Camillo's response ('True, but she loathes / I should be seen in't,' ll. 60–1) is probably an accidental innuendo on his part. The references to bowling – a popular pastime in Jacobean England – would have implied further continuity between the far-removed Italian world of the play and the Jacobean present (ll. 63–8).

75–86 Here the exchange becomes fast-paced, peppered with shared lines. Flamineo interrupts Camillo, steering his thought process, and deliberately confusing him by suggesting first one thing ('lock up your wife', l. 79) and then its opposite ('women are more willingly and more gloriously chaste when they are least restrained of their liberty', ll. 90–2). The pace of the dialogue suggests motion – perhaps Camillo's movement is quite literally steered by Flamineo here.

87–113 As Flamineo settles back into the role of misogynistic malcontent, the scene slips back into prose. His dominance of the conversation here suggests that he has come much closer to overcoming Camillo's resistance: the fast-paced activity of the previous exchange has probably now subsided. His metaphor of jealousy as a pair of spectacles which generate optical illusions (ll. 99–107) introduces a key theme: perspective and illusion.

114–45 Vittoria returns to the stage. Since the scene so far has revolved around discussions of this character, the audience might reasonably expect that she will now speak for herself. For now, however, she remains virtually silent and gives very little away.

Played well, Flamineo's conversation with Vittoria can be very funny. Partly (but not completely) within earshot of Camillo, it is the first of two 'overhearing' sequences in this scene. From line 123 onwards, Flamineo alternates loudly-spoken lines – designed for Camillo's hearing – with hushed asides (generally insults about Camillo) intended only for Vittoria's ears. The vivid metaphors with which Flamineo describes Camillo evoke dirt, fire and animals (particularly striking is his characterization of Camillo as a 'maggot', l. 142), and set a dark tone in which images of the hellish and the animalistic abound.

The audience will see Flamineo move from Camillo's side to Vittoria's, presenting a visual emblem of Vittoria's complicity with her brother, and of their ostracization of Camillo. The sequence presents certain staging difficulties: Flamineo's secret asides are presumably shared with both Vittoria and the audience, and would therefore be delivered downstage, and away from Camillo; but Camillo's commentary, in which he communicates to the audience his complete misreading of Flamineo and Vittoria's conversation, also implies proximity to the audience. To complicate things further, Flamineo clearly overhears Camillo's aside on line 148. It may be that they occupy opposite sides of the stage, and that Flamineo's ability to hear other characters' asides is conventional.

146–61 Flamineo's orchestration of his sister's adultery takes on a rather uncomfortable tone here. He moves on to describe Bracciano and Vittoria's imaged sexual union, and his language is now dominated by images of luxury and intoxication. His words are almost seductive. Vittoria (whom we have heard speak for herself only twice so far in the play, and both times chastely) is told 'thou shalt go to bed to my lord' (l. 146-7), and does not appear to have much of a say in the matter. Flamineo's subsequent *double entendre* to the unsuspecting Camillo – 'I am opening your case hard' (l. 150) – casts Flamineo himself in the role of the sexual aggressor, making him (symbolically, at least) his own sister's seducer. An audience's complicity with Flamineo may be strained by this passage, though he will probably continue to generate laughter.

162   This aside is the first textual indication we have of Vittoria's willingness to commit adultery – though in performance, this can be implied much earlier.

163–98   Flamineo successfully manipulates Camillo into allowing himself to be cuckolded, to the extent that Camillo himself insists Flamineo lock him in his bedchamber. The 'jest of the silkworm' of which Camillo is so proud (ll. 180–1,194) is turned against him by both Vittoria (l. 183) and Flamineo (ll. 197–8). The sense of the audience's own collusion in Camillo's victimization will be strengthened if they laugh at these lines.

199–269   Now the scene changes tone again, as Bracciano re-enters and re-establishes the iambic pentameter very conspicuously with a rhyming couplet (ll. 204–5). He and Vittoria speak the language of courtly love to one another, but they tend to talk in innuendoes and riddles rather than passionately.

Zanche rearranges the playing space so that its focal point becomes a luxurious carpet and cushions. Bracciano and Vittoria presumably either sit or lie down upon these, in close proximity to one another – lines 214 and 261 suggest a physical embrace. The stage picture will almost certainly bear an erotic charge, with connotations of illicit sex.

Cornelia's simultaneous entrance ('listening, behind') serves to re-contextualize Vittoria and Flamineo: they are somebody's children, and their actions will bring undeserved dishonour to a whole family.

214–21   This part of the scene introduces a network of observers, each providing a different perspective on the action: Flamineo and Zanche watch Bracciano and Vittoria at a distance, while Cornelia, in turn, sees all four. The audience, of course, observe all five. Cornelia speaks to the audience only once before she later reveals her presence to the other characters (ll. 216–21), but her silent (and presumably horrified) presence as an onstage observer goes no small way towards steering the audience's response to the scene. These various levels of 'watching' frame the scene as highly meta-theatrical and aware of its own artifice.

Flamineo's asides throughout this sequence may be directed squarely at the audience; a production might choose, however, to have him direct some at Zanche, with whom we know he has a rapport, and with whom we will later discover he has had an affair. His command to her on line 271 implies that they are close in proximity to one another by this point.

222–9 Vittoria and Bracciano's discussion of their 'jewels' is literal, but also a very thinly veiled discussion of their forthcoming sexual encounter. Flamineo, ever the debasing influence, ensures with two bawdy asides that this *double entendre* does not go unnoticed by the audience. The business of exchanging jewels also implies physical contact between the two leads, and this may be sexualized: Bracciano's insistence that Vittoria should wear his jewel 'lower' (l. 228) suggests some kind of sexual contact, as either he or she moves the jewel down her body.

230–56 Vittoria's account of her 'foolish idle dream' (l. 232) provides another change in tone, and makes it clear that Vittoria is just as clever and manipulative as her brother. The imagery of the scene moves suddenly from the heat of lust to the coldness of death: her metaphors here are overwhelmingly ones of decay and burial. The tone becomes much more sinister.

Bracciano does not, perhaps, understand straight away that she is talking in code; Vittoria, however, insists on the word 'yew' to such an extent that the audience can be left in little doubt as to her double meaning. Her presentation of Isabella as 'fell' (cruel and angry; l. 246) and 'like a Fury' (an avenging spirit in classical mythology; l. 247) contrasts with the passive and virtuous Isabella we will see in the very next scene.

257–9 Once again, Flamineo spells out the implications of Vittoria's speech in an aside to the audience. The line also links her with the 'devil' of the play's title.

260–9 As he interprets Vittoria's dream, Bracciano promises to 'seat' Vittoria 'above scandal', suggesting he intends to marry her and make her his duchess (ll. 264, 268–9). Neither Vittoria nor Bracciano has mentioned explicitly how they intend to dispose of their current spouses, however.

270–302   Cornelia chooses this moment to step forward. Her appearance shatters the careful artifice of the previous sequence and the scene explodes into full-blown confrontation. She is unafraid to breach etiquette and condemn her social superior as an 'adulterous duke' (l. 285). Her use of *sententiae* (ll. 282–3, 289–90 and 300–1) establishes her as a moral force, though one might wonder whether her observations as to the way in which 'princes' should behave are somewhat naïve; certainly none of the play's politically powerful characters demonstrate such virtue.

This sequence is full of interruptions, shared lines and incomplete sentences, as the characters clamour to be heard over one another. Lines 294–5 imply that Vittoria is kneeling down before her mother, who sinks to join her, adding to the fast-paced physical business. Vittoria's exit is sudden and unceremonious.

Cornelia's revelation that Isabella has arrived in Rome (l. 286) prompts shocked reactions from Flamineo, Vittoria and Bracciano alike: all three share one line (l. 287), and Bracciano is cut off mid-flow. Both this, and the first line of Flamineo's soliloquy at the end of the scene (l. 347), anticipate the trouble which will be caused by Isabella's arrival; it is likely that the audience will now be eager to see this key character introduced.

303–8   Bracciano resolves to speak to Doctor Julio (presumably with murder in mind) and anticipates a 'fearful and prodigious storm' and 'ensuing harm' (ll. 307–8). He pre-emptively blames it upon Cornelia's intervention, already attempting to disavow his own responsibility.

309–46   Flamineo's dialogue with his mother exemplifies a clash between two very different perspectives: one cynical and sarcastic, the other honourable and outraged. Cornelia's insistence upon honour, argues Flamineo, ignores the necessity of moral compromise in order to advance in life (ll. 309–15). Cornelia points out that poverty is no excuse for vice (ll. 315–**16**). The argument is not a balanced one, however: Flamineo makes his point at length, pointing bitterly to his father's squandered riches, his own lost inheritance, and the time he has spent in one sort of service or another (and his ambiguous reference to 'conspiring with a beard' on line 324 suggests an unexplained but distinctly unwholesome back-story).

Cornelia does not attempt to argue, but simply wishes aloud that her son had never been born (l. 334). He disowns her in return (ll. 334–6). These are terrible things for a mother and son to say to one another, and there may be a sense that both characters have just done irrevocable damage to their relationship.

347–55   Flamineo's soliloquy at the end of the scene, spoken directly to the audience, cements his position both as a scheming malcontent and as the closest character to the audience in the play so far. His choice of metaphors implies an affinity with the lawless world of nature rather than the moral systems of civilization. The line 'We are engaged to mischief and must on' (l. 348) is ambiguous: Flamineo's 'we' may refer to Flamineo and Vittoria, Flamineo and Bracciano, all three of them, or indeed Flamineo and the audience.

Act II

Act II, scene i

This long and important scene introduces the audience to a second group of central characters: Francisco, Monticelso and Isabella. With its busy stage, secret scheming, and interplay of public and private, it is in many ways a mirror image of the previous scene. This scene is full of characters expressing ideas which are contrary to what they really feel. It allows the audience more insight into Bracciano's character, and sets up the action of the next scene, in which we will see both Camillo and Isabella murdered on his orders. The scene also raises questions about the motivation behind Francisco's ruthless pursuit of Vittoria and Bracciano: though he is ostensibly concerned with the protection of his family's honour, he is clearly willing to manipulate circumstances so that Bracciano and Vittoria *will* commit adultery. Lines 84–91 indicate that Francisco and Bracciano are engaged in a covert battle for power, status and influence, and hint at ulterior motives.

1–10   The opening of the scene clearly establishes Isabella, Francisco and Giovanni's relations to one another (and to the absent Bracciano). It is made immediately clear to us that Isabella is the duchess we heard so much about in the previous scene. Giovanni is probably a young child, so his presence with Isabella establishes a picture of her as an icon of motherhood. This contrasts strongly with the fractured mother–child relationships we saw in the previous scene.

Our first impression of Francisco is likely to be one of a much less peaceful character. His startling image of setting fire to Bracciano's 'dove-house' (l. 3) suggests a propensity towards violence, while his reference to 'pole-cats' (l. 5) would have been recognized by Webster's audience as a slang term for prostitutes, and is strong language to refer to the high-ranking Bracciano and Vittoria.

Two other significant characters share the stage here. Marcello is introduced, but interestingly Webster chooses *not* to establish yet that he is brother to Vittoria and Flamineo – clearly we are meant to see him first and foremost as a dutiful servant to Francisco, and will discover his family connections only later in the play. More importantly, this sequence also introduces Monticelso to the stage, but he remains silent until he is invited to speak by Francisco at line 20. Monticelso is a powerful figure – he will later become Pope, and his costume will presumably make it immediately clear to the audience that he is a high-ranking Cardinal – so his silence will be striking. He may be a conspicuous brooding presence in this opening sequence, commanding the audience's attention as the other characters talk amongst themselves.

10–18   Isabella's first significant speech is markedly at odds with Vittoria's characterization of her in the previous scene as 'like a Fury' (I.ii.247). Here, she asks her brother to speak 'mildly' to her husband (l. 11). Her suggestion that she will 'force' Bracciano to be faithful, however (l. 17) – and her description of his affair as 'an infected straying' (l. 18) – might imply a more vehement feeling than the speech expresses superficially. In performance, Isabella might be played as a woman who is struggling to maintain her composure in the face of her husband's open infidelity.

19   In just one line, Webster radically alters the stage picture. Isabella leaves, Bracciano and Flamineo enter, and then all but

Bracciano, Francisco and Monticelso vacate the stage. This sudden emptying of a busy space recalls the beginning of I.ii, and (just as it did in that scene) marks a shift from public to private. The audience are now primed to expect an 'unofficial', off-the-record conversation. Francisco's abrupt command – 'Void the chamber' – demonstrates his unassailable authority in this scene, and may contain an element of menace.

20–5 On the surface, the three onstage characters are entirely polite to one another here. Bracciano is invited to sit; then Monticelso speaks for the first time in what might seem a reasonable and considered manner, and Bracciano acquiesces to his request. In performance, however, the exchange may be imbued with tension – does Bracciano sit, as requested? If he does, do Francisco and Monticelso sit too, or do they remain standing? Do they position themselves either side of him (in a visual echo of I.i, perhaps)?

26–44 Monticelso's speech is long, eloquent and uninterrupted. Ostensibly he is making a calm appeal for Bracciano to repent his unprincely actions; his use of words like 'insatiate' and 'lascivious', however, suggest a more emotive aspect to the speech (ll. 32, 35). When Bracciano begins to respond – presumably to defend himself – Monticelso interrupts him almost immediately, efficiently asserting his own status. This is clearly a man used to choosing for himself when he will and will not speak.

45–51 Bracciano decides (probably on the basis of this last interruption) not to argue with Monticelso, but rather to challenge Francisco to speak up: perhaps he senses that he can engage the latter in debate on more equal terms. Line 47 gives an indication that Bracciano and Francisco's conversation is likely to be much more combative – the two speakers share a single line of iambic pentameter, both speaking entirely in punchy monosyllables. Francisco continues Bracciano's alliteration ('Do not fear it'), and then turns Bracciano's 'own hawking phrase' back upon him (l. 48), in the first of many metaphors in the play which compare its characters with birds of prey (see also IV.ii.83, V.i.186, V.iv.4–9, and V.vi.184–6). The language of the two characters – evenly matched and equally aggressive – suggests both a short-term conflict and an emerging long-term power struggle.

52–79   Monticelso stays entirely silent throughout this fiery quarrel between the two Dukes. Bracciano and Francisco trade words almost as if they were blows – virtually every new speech begins mid-line, often as an interruption of the previous speaker, and several threats are exchanged. It is hard to imagine that Bracciano could remain seated through this; if he did indeed sit when requested to do so on line 20, this sequence may provide the opportunity for a physical 'explosion' as he rises from his chair in anger. It is significant that he appeals to the silent Monticelso on line 56 in his attempt to mock (and presumably discredit) Francisco's implication of impropriety.

80–94   Monticelso once again asserts his authority in order to bring the argument to a temporary truce. Francisco complains of Bracciano's unwillingness to meet him in order to discuss 'levies 'gainst the pirates' (l. 85), suggesting that his grudge against Bracciano may be founded upon more than just the latter's infidelity. He retreats into riddles which hint at Bracciano's sexual corruption – a marked change from his earlier overt assertions ('She is your strumpet', l. 58) and open threats ('We'll end this with the cannon', l. 73). Has he been unnerved?

95–144   The entrance of young Giovanni – Bracciano's son and Francisco's nephew – diffuses the hostile mood immediately, as Bracciano and Francisco join together to comment upon Giovanni's innocent charm. Francisco speaks much more than Bracciano – an indication, perhaps, that the latter's relationship with his son is not everything it could be. Francisco's rapport with Giovanni is important – these two characters will survive the play, and the relationship between them shown here may give us a hint as to the kind of power balance that will be established in Italy following the play's conclusion. Casting Giovanni presents modern productions with a potential problem: too young, and Giovanni becomes implausibly (and perhaps irritatingly) precocious; too old, and as Emrys Jones has pointed out, this scene 'becomes ridiculous', while the character's second scene (III.ii.310–41) 'loses its pathos' (1991: 17).

This exchange provides another perspective on the play's debates surrounding appropriate 'princely' behaviour. Where Cornelia voiced a romanticized ideal about 'the lives of princes' in I.ii (ll. 288–90), Monticelso has argued here that Bracciano's current behaviour will endanger his 'princely title' (ll. 37–42). Now, Giovanni imagines himself as a brave and warlike but merciful leader in the mould of many of the 'princely' heroes of the Renaissance stage (one might be reminded, for example, of Shakespeare's *Henry V*). Giovanni may have been a portrait of the real-life Prince Henry, son to James I, about whom Webster would go on to write an elegy when the Prince died in late 1612 (*A Monumental Column*). Henry was popularly seen as a noble, warlike and highly religious counterpoint to his father's sycophantic and decadent court, and his death was widely mourned. To the Jacobean audience, then, a child clad in armour may have been a powerful symbol of chivalry and virtue.

The sequence concludes with an apparently amicable end to Francisco and Bracciano's dispute, as the two share one line which asserts their mutual friendship (l. 139). We discover later in the scene that neither party was at all sincere in this. Francisco's lines about Lodovico are a seemingly inconsequential afterthought; the actor playing Francisco might consider that the character is setting up an elaborate trap for Bracciano by finding an excuse to send Camillo away, and that this is the first that we (and Bracciano) hear of it.

144–6 Once again, the stage picture rapidly changes. Isabella enters and is left alone with Bracciano, who promises the departing Francisco that he will treat her kindly. We soon see that Bracciano has no intention of keeping his word.

147–79 Bracciano attempts to accuse his wife of adultery, rudely rejecting her entreaties of love. This is when Isabella is likely to make her biggest impression on an audience. Webster has led us to expect trouble: news of her arrival in Rome provoked agitation amongst the protagonists in the previous scene, and despite her calmness at the beginning of this scene, there have been hints of a more passionate side to her. The fact that she maintains her composure over this exchange, as Bracciano provokes her ever further, might serve to increase the audience's anticipation of her inevitable breaking-point.

180–92 Bracciano resumes his former hostility towards Francisco, cursing and insulting him. His speech contains the scene's second reference to the importance of costume and outward appearance – where Francisco, earlier on, read much into Vittoria's 'cloth of tissue'

(l. 54), Bracciano suggests here that Francisco's power and authority derives solely from 'his wardrobe' and 'his robes of state' (ll. 185–6). He then turns his curse onto the priest who married him to Isabella, and finally onto his own son, prompting Isabella to object. Having just seen Bracciano treating the same son with affection, we are likely to agree with Isabella that he has cursed 'too too far' (l. 92). If Isabella has been played until this point as a passive victim, it will be difficult to sustain any longer: she speaks now as an outraged mother.

193–209   Just as he has provoked his strongest reaction from his wife, Bracciano now performs an inverted parody of the wedding ceremony as he promises to divorce her. The text requires him to kiss (or at least attempt to kiss) Isabella's hand: her reaction to this physical invasion will be interesting. Quite what Bracciano does with his wedding ring when he swears by it is unclear: he might leave it on, take it off, thrust it at Isabella, or even throw it. Whatever he does with it will be loaded with meaning, since the ring is a physical symbol of his marriage vows.

Lines 208–9 draw particular attention to the word 'Never'. Isabella asks Bracciano – perhaps in incredulity, perhaps in anger – to repeat his vow. Bracciano, in a striking abandonment of the scene's iambic pentameter, answers simply by repeating the word. The metric irregularity implies a short silence before the next line is spoken: this will focus our attention on Isabella's temporarily silent response.

210–25   Isabella reacts calmly and selflessly, taking Bracciano's sins upon herself, and promising to give her brother the impression that the divorce was her own desire. Her passivity, and her apparent willingness to sacrifice all for her unloving husband, are difficult for the modern performer to reconcile with today's gender politics – it might be hard to imagine what the character's motivation for taking this course of action could be. It may be worth considering, though, that Isabella's 'performance' of her 'sad ensuing part' (l. 225) will allow her to give voice to a 'just anger' (l. 250) which might not otherwise have found expression.

226–45   Francisco and the others return to find Isabella weeping. We, the audience, know something they do not – that she is now performing a 'part'. How much of her behaviour, then, is sincere, and how much is pretence? Can we even tell the difference? Isabella lies to her brother when she swears that Bracciano was not 'loud' in their private exchange (ll. 235–6). When she wishes that she 'were a man', though – that she might have 'power / To execute my apprehended wishes' (ll. 243–4) – we might sense a more genuine expression of her frustration at the gender inequality which put her in this position in the first place.

245–51 Isabella now becomes the 'Fury' (l. 245) which was antici-pated by Vittoria earlier in the play (I.ii.247). Her fantasies of violence towards Vittoria are indeed ferocious: not only in their physical cruelty (striking as this is) but also in the words themselves. Vittoria is described as a 'strumpet', and Isabella draws on images of putrefac-tion to describe her rival's body (ll. 248–9). Her language is sibilant – spoken aloud, lines 244–50 will sound a lot like spitting.

It will be impossible for an audience to differentiate between Isabella's 'performance' and her true feelings here (since in theatre, the latter are embodied only through performance anyway). As so often in this play, we are presented with ambiguous behaviour, the true motives of which we are left simply to guess at. The vehemence of the language, however, suggests sincerity.

251–63 Isabella uses Bracciano's exact words in order to 'perform' the divorce he enacted only moments ago. Is this an attempt to embarrass him, or perhaps to make him feel guilty? Will the audi-ence laugh as they recognize that Bracciano's own words are being used against him? Maybe Isabella is attempting to out-perform her husband: it is significant that while she quotes Bracciano accurately over most of these lines, his promise that the divorce will be 'as truly kept / As if the judge had doomed it' (ll. 196–7) becomes, in her mouth, 'as truly kept / As if in thronged court a thousand ears / Had heard it and a thousand lawyers' hands / Sealed to the separation' (ll. 256–9). In the theatre, this may well draw attention to the 'thousand ears' of the audience themselves, who have indeed borne witness to the divorce.

This sequence also offers its actors the opportunity to repeat and re-inscribe the physical gestures which marked Bracciano's divorce vow only moments before. How does Isabella kiss Bracciano? Does she repeat whatever gestures Bracciano may have made in reference to his ring? There is likely to be strong element of visual irony here.

264–78   Francisco is quick to blame his sister for this turn of events. His repetition of Bracciano's earlier command to Isabella – 'take your chamber' (ll. 154 and 269) – reinforces the impression that the two men have resolved their differences and united against Isabella. Francisco's anticipation of the 'excellent laughter' that the men will share when she comes to regret her 'rash vow' (l. 276) strikes an ugly and misogynistic note. Isabella's aside as she leaves, however, positions her closest to the audience in this scene (and her implied reference to the audience on lines 256–9 may have had the same effect). The men may have ganged up against her, but we are likely to be inclined to take her part.

279–311   Camillo's entrance marks the beginning of a split-stage sequence, in which he, Francisco, Monticelso and Marcello presumably move to the rear of the playing space in order to 'whisper' about the commission (l. 283), while Bracciano and Flamineo conspire together at the front with Doctor Julio. Bracciano and Flamineo lapse into prose as they discuss underhand matters, just as they did in I.ii. Flamineo's coarse humour is once again likely to make an audience laugh; he is bringing Bracciano closer to the audience, both literally and metaphorically.

312–22   Just as Flamineo is entering full satirical flow, Bracciano commands 'No more' (l. 312) and moves the dialogue back into verse, shifting away from the world of the audience and back to the world of the plot. Flamineo, Bracciano and Doctor Julio depart the scene leaving the audience anticipating bloody action: Camillo and Isabella are to be murdered.

323–56   Our attention shifts to the other onstage conversation, which will probably now move forwards. Monticelso presents Camillo with an 'emblem' of a weeping stag, which he claims was thrown in at his nephew's window – the drawing supposedly symbolizes Camillo's status as a 'horned' cuckold. Since we have already learned to recognize Camillo as an easily manipulated fool, however, an audience may well suspect here that the emblem is Monticelso's own device: a suspicion which his behaviour later in this scene will serve only to reinforce. The quotation from Ovid's *Metamorphoses* puzzles Camillo, who turns, trustingly, to his uncle for explanation.

Francisco then complements Monticelso's manipulation of Camillo by offering a similarly oblique riddle – in this case, a retelling of one of Aesop's fables, the significance of which becomes apparent only at its conclusion. Camillo's short half-lines throughout these exchanges show him to be confused and easily led, while his companions' classical allusions illustrate their intelligence and sophistication.

357–69 Having bewildered and unsettled Camillo, Francisco and Monticelso present his commission to 'relieve our Italian coast / From pirates' (ll. 361–2) as if it were a solution to his problems. Camillo sees the flaw in this logic – that his absence will surely encourage Vittoria's infidelity rather than prevent it – but is rapidly assured otherwise. He leaves the stage with an uneasy bravado.

370–93 We now see another facet to princely conduct, as Francisco and Monticelso behave in a manner much like Machiavelli's conception of 'The Prince' (see 'Renaissance Italy on the Jacobean stage', Chapter 3). Depending on the way in which Monticelso has been played thus far, this final section of the scene will come either as a shocking twist or as a confirmation of our suspicions; Monticelso has, after all, been conspiring with Francisco, and does not have his nephew's interests at heart at all. They have stage-managed events so that Bracciano and Vittoria *will* commit adultery, and hope to lead them into 'notorious scandal' (l. 383). The scene gives only hints as to their motivations for this: family honour is the explicit reason, but both seem relatively contemptuous of their own wronged relatives. Lines 84–7 in particular suggest there may be a wider political dimension to their actions.

The reference to Lodovico in Padua suggests the way in which the charismatic ruffian introduced to us in the play's first scene will become involved in the unfolding plot. The image of poisonous rot as the scene concludes (ll. 397–8) echoes several others from earlier (see lines 51, 246–50, and 299–311). The cumulative effect creates a sense of profound unease.

Act II, scene ii

This scene takes place in Camillo's house, but is not identified as such until lines 50–1. In effect, then, this scene might seem to an audience to be set in an unspecified limbo; this eerie and unsettling displacement can only be intensified when the similarly mysterious and nameless Conjuror summons up visions of the recently murdered Isabella and Camillo. The sequence has a potentially disconcerting, otherworldly effect.

The dumb-show was a familiar convention in Renaissance drama, but by the time Webster wrote this play, it was a distinctly old-fashioned device. Perhaps it is here simply in order to compress the action of what could have been three scenes into one, thus maintaining the play's pace and tension. There may be more to it, however. Arguably, the stylized dumb-shows create a distancing effect akin to the twentieth-century dramatist Bertolt Brecht's 'alienation effect', pulling us away from any sympathy we might otherwise have felt for Isabella and Camillo, and turning our attention towards Bracciano's reactions. The scene thus serves to turn the audience against Bracciano, casting him – not Vittoria – as the instigator of the violence. The sequence should therefore have a direct impact upon the audience's perception of Vittoria's guilt – or otherwise – in the forthcoming trial scene.

1–4   When we see first him, we do not know who the Conjuror is. His costume, however, marks him out as someone with supernatural (and therefore, for the Jacobean audience, damnable) powers. We learn that it is midnight, a time with particularly rich symbolic associations for the Jacobean audience: many believed that the spirits of the dead would leave their graves and walk, and the hour was associated with witchcraft.

5–23   The Conjuror seems oddly reluctant to practise his 'art', claiming that he would 'gladly lose' the name of 'nigromancer' (a dark magician who speaks with the dead). He has been persuaded by Bracciano's 'bounty' – in other words, bribed – providing another example of the moral compromises that rich and powerful men can force their social inferiors to make. In a further illustration of the play's themes of deceit and corruption, the Conjuror describes

the 'tricks' of charlatans and fraudsters who merely pretend to have
supernatural powers. He invites Bracciano to put on a 'charmed'
night-cap (anticipating, perhaps, the method of Bracciano's own
murder later in the play) and promises to show him Isabella's death.
His description of her broken heart (l. 23) is particularly poignant
given Bracciano's most recent description of her as his 'loathed
duchess' (l. 4).

23 s.d.   Suddenly, the play moves into a different register of performance. At the Red Bull, the dumb-shows were probably revealed in the
'discovery space' – a small room at the back of the stage, hidden by
a curtain. The audience are shown a sequence of action which is
entirely mimed, and which is presumably accompanied by music
from below the stage (as implied in line 36). The play's storytelling
thus becomes much more stylized; this alone is likely to make it
unsettling to watch.

The audience are confronted with yet another unfamiliar character – in this case, Dr Julio's assistant (named 'Christophero' in
Webster's text) – which may add another element of disorientation.
The first two characters we see are embodiments of pure evil: Julio
and his assistant wear *'spectacles of glass, which cover their eyes and noses'*,
distorting their facial features and making them appear inhuman
(even demonic). Further hellish connotations are added by the flames
they light (an inverted version, perhaps, of the incense used in religious ceremonies), and by their laughing departure.

Isabella enters and provides a marked visual contrast. Wearing
a nightgown and kneeling down to pray, she is innocent, pious and
vulnerable. As she kisses the painting of her husband, the audience may be reminded of the kiss of divorce which took place in
the previous scene. Her death by poison once again foreshadows
Bracciano's death later in the play.

The stage direction describes *'sorrow expressed in Giovanni and in
Count Lodovico'*. Depending on the style of the dumb-show, this may
be either moving or so divorced from realism that the audience
are unable to empathize. Lodovico's reaction – particularly given
the references to his presence in Padua at the end of the previous
scene – may allow the audience to guess at the information revealed
a few lines later: that he 'did most passionately dote' upon Isabella
(l. 31). It is likely to contrast with Bracciano's reaction as he watches,

underlining the Duke's cruelty: the first word he speaks in response to what he sees now is 'Excellent' (l. 24).

24–37 The Conjuror solicits sympathy for Isabella here as he explains her 'custom' of visiting Bracciano's picture every night – Julio's actions seem all the more callous as we realize that Isabella's devotion has been exploited and turned against her. The description of Bracciano's picture as a 'dead shadow' is foreboding, while the information regarding Lodovico's previously un-indicated love for Isabella gives another motivation for his later actions.

37 s.d. The second dumb-show is even more extreme than the first: more spectacular, accompanied by 'louder music' (l. 36), and depicting a 'far more politic' (craftier) murder (l. 35). It is significant that Webster chooses to present, as the climax to this scene, the death of the *least* sympathetic of the two victims – whereas we have been encouraged to sympathize with Isabella, we have probably been encouraged to laugh at Camillo. Here, given Camillo's (probably unconvincing) macho posturing and Flamineo's unashamed and brazen treachery, it may be that even Camillo's murder provokes laughter in performance. On the other hand, the physical display involved can make the scene spectacular and thrilling.

The heightened gestural and facial style of the dumb-show form may allow us to differentiate between the genuine 'sorrow' of Giovanni and Lodovico, Flamineo's phony 'shows' of concern, Marcello's 'lament', and Monticelso and Francisco's 'wonder at the act'. The latter will be particularly interesting to watch, given their dismissive manipulation of Camillo in the previous scene.

38–50 Once again, the Conjuror interprets the action of the dumb-show for the benefit of both Bracciano and the audience. He is careful to point out that Marcello is 'virtuous' and 'innocent' (ll. 43, 44) and that he has been unfairly arrested along with Flamineo. We remain unaware that Marcello and Flamineo are brothers.

The Conjuror's dispassionate descriptions of both murders will have an unsettling effect upon the audience. Are we encouraged to share his detachment, or does it make the whole scene even more unpalatable?

50–5 This oddly supernatural and dreamlike scene is reincorporated seamlessly into the play's realism with the Conjuror's revelation that 'we are now / Beneath her [Vittoria's] roof' (ll. 50–1) – perhaps his 'we' includes the audience as well as himself and Bracciano. Vittoria's impending arrest, and the possibility that Bracciano will be discovered in her house, adds urgency. Bracciano departs the scene still in debt to the Conjuror (who, we should remember, agreed to help Bracciano only in order that he might be paid).

56–7 The Conjuror's final couplet once again takes the form of a *sententia*, and implies his disapproval of Bracciano's actions.

Act III

Act III, scene i

This short, bustling scene keeps the audience in suspense. Having witnessed the events of II.ii, we will be anticipating both the discovery by Francisco and Monticelso of Isabella's death, and the outcome of Vittoria's arrest (we learn within seconds that she is to be put on trial). Both, however, are delayed for the moment. Once again, we find ourselves in a private, unofficial space, adjacent to a public and official one.

1–10 This brief exchange between Francisco and Monticelso is very much an unofficial one, giving the audience a glimpse into their behind-the-scenes political manoeuvring. Francisco reveals that Monticelso has 'dealt discreetly' to ensure that Vittoria's trial is witnessed by a large number of high-ranking foreign dignitaries (l. 1), while Monticelso explains that this is to ensure that Vittoria's reputation is ruined as publicly as possible. He admits that they have nothing but circumstantial evidence with which to charge her; the trial is thus a political move rather than a legal obligation. It is also notable that the trial has been recast as one concerning Vittoria's 'black lust' (l. 7) rather than the murder of Camillo.

The two silent figures – the Chancellor and Register – lurk ominously in the background. Both are officials of the court. It may be that they are simply listening to their superiors, but it will probably be more dramatically effective if they are preparing the stage space for the forthcoming trial while their superiors confer conspiratorially in the foreground.

11–29   Another group of characters enters the stage, adding to the scene's sense of bustle and activity; it may be that if the Chancellor and Register are indeed setting up the space for the trial, they remain in the background here.

The switch into prose makes it clear that both Flamineo and the Lawyer are speaking the relaxed, informal language of unofficial culture. Most of the jokes are simple innuendoes, but the quibbling over the terms 'private' and 'public' plays on one of the play's key themes – the discrepancy between public and private behaviour.

Both Flamineo and Marcello are guarded, but they form a visual contrast here: while Flamineo jokes at length with the Lawyer, Marcello is conspicuously silent. His reactions to these bawdy quips will be interesting to watch, especially since they concern his own sister (though the audience do not yet know this). Though it is not indicated in a stage direction, it would make theatrical sense for the Lawyer to leave Flamineo and Marcello (and perhaps the stage) at line 29: this would make their conversation below a more private one, and explain the sudden change in tone.

30–1   Flamineo re-establishes his close relationship with the audience in this aside, revealing that his apparent light-heartedness is merely a ruse so that he might avoid suspicion. It is striking that it is this intimate revelation which moves the scene back into verse: hinting, perhaps, that Flamineo's 'unofficial' speech masks a well-hidden dignity.

31–6   This short but important passage reveals a great deal for the first time about Marcello. Most importantly, we learn that he is Vittoria's brother (and therefore also Flamineo's). His stated wish that Vittoria should have died 'When she first saw Bracciano' (l. 34) associates him with conventional Jacobean morality, and his attack on Flamineo sets up a comparison between two brothers who are in many senses paired opposites: where one is honourable, moralistic and outspoken, the other is duplicitous, amoral and deceptive. If we think we know with which of the pair we are meant to sympathize, however, we may be surprised by the passage which follows.

36–63 This debate between the two brothers is strongly reminiscent of I.ii.309–46, in which Flamineo and Cornelia argued over the ethics of moral compromise. Like his mother, Marcello fails to put up an adequate defence for traditional morality, barely managing to interrupt his unscrupulous but eloquent brother. Once again, Flamineo makes the case for a kind of ruthless individualism, pointing out that loyalty and good service have got Marcello nowhere. When Marcello finally does speak up, his advice is conventional, but it also warns of the dangers of the court; this sentiment will be echoed by other characters later in the play. Flamineo agrees to 'think on't' (l. 63).

64–78 Flamineo resumes his appearance of cheerfulness (and the disguise of prose) as the Ambassadors enter for Vittoria's trial, and he is rejoined by the Lawyer. As they mock the Ambassadors, Flamineo and the Lawyer once again exchange sexual innuendoes; what has come before, however, might encourage an audience to see a more troubled Flamineo beneath this humorous façade.

Act III, scene ii

The fact that this scene is given its own title – 'The Arraignment of Vittoria' – is an indication of its importance within the play's structure. It is in many senses the midway point, the hinge of the plot. It is the only scene to feature all of the central characters. Dramaturgically, we are positioned on Vittoria's side: she is powerful and defiant, her opponents corrupt and unfair. Bracciano's blasé presence, and his silence when things become difficult for Vittoria, highlight the injustice of her situation and add dramatic tension.

The dynamics of the scene shift rapidly. Quick, fiery arguments are interspersed with longer, rhetorical speeches; anger alternates with craft, and, towards the end, humorous prose with heartfelt grief. Monticelso and Francisco swap roles here, so that Monticelso becomes the one with the fiery temper and Francisco the voice of moderation. The Ambassadors are called upon to 'look' and 'mark' throughout the scene – as are the audience, who are asked to judge not only Vittoria, but also those who sit in judgement over her.

The scene could be played as a continuous extension of the previous scene, marking a sudden switch from private to public. If Flamineo, Marcello, the Lawyer and the Ambassadors stay on stage, the transition gains a sense of building anticipation as the 'audience' for the trial amass; if they exit, on the other hand, then their subsequent re-entrance as part of a larger group emphasizes their increasing marginalization.

1–7 It is important to think about the stage picture here. In his 'Theatrical Introduction' to the play, David Carnegie uses a woodcut from the title page of *Swetnam the Woman-Hater* (see 'Women and misogyny', Chapter 3) to make inferences about how trial scenes would have been staged at the Red Bull. He concludes that Monticelso, as judge, would be 'seated on a raised state, placed centrally and well back towards the tiring-house wall'. Vittoria, meanwhile, 'will be standing facing him at some distance, separated by a table and almost certainly a bar'. The Ambassadors would sit on stools on one side, and Francisco, the Chancellor and the Register on the other, to create an enclosed rectangle. Though this configuration would be impractical in a modern proscenium-arch theatre (Vittoria would have her back to the audience), in a Jacobean playhouse with audience members on all sides it would actually work very dynamically. The accused, notes Carnegie, 'is in a strong position to play to the gallery (as Vittoria clearly does)' (1995: 103).

In modern spaces, the scene tends to be played with Vittoria occupying a fairly static central position, facing the audience; Monticelso may have a seat somewhere upstage, but is likely to move out of it. Such a configuration will emphasize the audience's role as judges. Alternatively, Vittoria and Monticelso can be presented on opposite sides of the space, suggesting a confrontation between characters who are equal and opposite. Modern stagings of this scene are explored further in Chapter 4.

The ordered stage picture is disrupted immediately by Bracciano, who sits himself down on the floor (presumably downstage). His abruptness and contempt for Monticelso's authority are conveyed by his brusque half-line (l. 3), while his response to Francisco is sarcastic (ll. 5–7). This opening sets up an uneasy tension between oppressive order and defiant subversion which underpins the rest of the scene.

8–25 The trial begins formally, as Monticelso addresses Vittoria with a feigned courtesy (though his use of 'gentlewoman' may be played sarcastically), and the Lawyer opens proceedings in Latin. Almost straight away, however, Vittoria interjects, establishing during a quick-fire exchange with Francisco that she wishes the case against her to be made in the language that 'this auditory' might understand (l. 15) – Italian, presumably, within the fictional world of the play (though most of the characters on stage would be educated enough to understand Latin), but in reality, of course, English. Monticelso's attempt to resume the trial (l. 17) is immediately interrupted again by Vittoria, and when he subsequently backs down – somewhat bad-temperedly – his authority is fatally undermined (ll. 22–3). Vittoria's suggestion that she is like a target at which the Lawyer might practise his archery implies that he is an incompetent amateur, 'aiming' in the wrong direction (ll. 24–5).

Vittoria's two references to the assembled audience (lines 15 and 19) may well be played (or indeed interpreted) as references to the real-life audience at the theatre. This may have the effect either of engaging the audience's sympathy, or of foregrounding our own role as observers and judges of her conduct; it may, of course, do both at once. It is significant that the 'offenders' in this scene – Vittoria and Bracciano – are both aligned in some way with the audience in the scene's dramaturgy.

26–50 Is this the same Lawyer we saw joking with Flamineo in the previous scene? In modern productions, limitations on cast size are likely to mean that the same actor plays both. In such cases, the Lawyer becomes another example of a character whose private personality is radically different from that which he presents in public. Here, his verbose and pretentious speech marks him out as a pompous charlatan who relies upon impenetrable language in order to maintain his status.

His use of nonsense and obscure terminology – such as 'literated' (l. 26), 'diversivolent' (l. 28) and 'exulceration' (l. 34) – is likely to make an audience laugh. Vittoria's witty description of his language (ll. 35–9) may well give voice to the audience's own feelings, and the

Lawyer barely manages to defend himself. Francisco dismisses him – at first with politeness, then scornfully – as the Duke realizes that the trial has started badly for the prosecution. As the Lawyer leaves the stage with another comically pretentious line, Francisco and Monticelso are left in a weakened position.

51–71 Monticelso drops the court's previous (and disastrous) attempts at formality, and speaks plainly and with vehemence. His initial reference to Vittoria's make-up (ll. 52–3) draws attention, once again, to the discrepancy between appearance and reality (and may, in the Jacobean theatre, have drawn attention to the artifice of the boy-actor playing Vittoria). Vittoria's deceptive exterior then becomes the theme of his attack. His description of her as a 'devil' once again links her with the play's title (see also I.ii.257), which is itself a reference to evil in the disguise of goodness.

Vittoria's defence, however, is robust. She asserts her own nobility (ll. 53–5) before pointing out the impropriety of Monticelso's willingness to 'play the lawyer' given his official role as judge (ll. 59–61). Her suggestion that cardinals are generally merciless (and her implication that they may often be corrupt) plays into an anti-Catholic sentiment which would have been rife amongst Webster's audience.

72–106 After citing some anecdotal and circumstantial evidence of Vittoria's colourful lifestyle, Monticelso really hits his stride with a scathing diatribe (which remains largely uninterrupted) against 'whores'. The speech is striking and memorable, with its repetitions of the question 'What are whores?' and its vivid metaphors of deceptive outward appearances and disguised corruption. This is a well-crafted piece of rhetoric, describing a particular character-type; writing of this sort was very popular in Jacobean England.

A close analysis of the passage reveals a subtle shift in tone. Monticelso's metaphors are straightforward and unembellished over the first few lines (ll. 79–82). After his first rhetorical question 'What are whores?', his metaphors become more complex, describing legal and state corruption (ll. 86–91). The speech builds in momentum as he repeats the question, and suddenly his images are increasingly emotional and visceral: funerals, extortion, riot, execution, corpses (ll. 92–8). His vehemence here – particularly given his measured language during his previous appearances in the play – hints at a man whose violent and sexual urges have been uneasily repressed, and find a nasty and unwholesome outlet in his role as punisher. His final repetition of the question subtly rephrases it: in asking 'What's a whore?', he allows himself to address a singular 'whore' rather than the plural. 'She's like the guilty counterfeited coin' (l. 99) seems to describe Vittoria in particular, rather than 'whores' in general. He has performed a cunning verbal sleight-of-hand.

It is worth noting that Monticelso's attack is composed entirely of rhetorical generalizations, and does not refer once to the specifics of Vittoria's conduct. As her terse reply (l. 101) suggests, Monticelso's speech is neither appropriate nor admissible as evidence in a courtroom.

106–7 The interjections of the two Ambassadors remind the audience of their own role in this scene: judging not only Vittoria's behaviour, but also Monticelso's. We may agree that Vittoria has 'livèd ill' (l. 106), or we may not – but it is fairly undeniable that Monticelso's conduct has been unduly biased and 'too bitter' (l. 107).

108–24 Monticelso and Francisco join forces to accuse Vittoria of complicity in Camillo's murder – though at no point does either say this outright. Both characters prefer to hint at her guilt obliquely, through irony and insinuation. Their multiple shared lines indicate that they are working as a team.

125–51 This passage shows Vittoria at her most eloquent and persuasive, and although we know she is at least *implicated* in Camillo's murder, we are likely to feel a great deal of sympathy for her. She points out that the trial is inordinately biased against her, and defends her very right to defend herself. When she argues that she must 'personate masculine virtue' in order to do this (l. 136), it might remind us of Isabella's wish in the previous act that she 'were a man' (II.i.243). The women in this world, the play seems to suggest, are stuck in an impossible double-bind: in order to achieve any kind of autonomy, they must become more 'masculine'; but if they attempt this, they will be condemned for it (see 'Women and misogyny', Chapter 3).

Vittoria's challenge to Monticelso to find her guilty and have her executed recalls the words of another Shakespearean character: those

of the innocent Hermione in *The Winter's Tale* (III.ii), who likewise
defies her tyrannical judge with a speech of strength and dignity.
One might also compare Queen Katherine's trial speech in II.iv.11–54
of *Henry VIII* (*All Is True*), a play of Shakespeare's which was written
at around the same time as *The White Devil*. The difference here is
that Vittoria is not entirely innocent – but dramaturgically, at least,
she is clearly playing the role of the defiant victim. The English
Ambassador, who spoke for the audience earlier on in the scene (l.
107), once again gives an indication as to how we are meant to view
this: like him, perhaps, we are supposed to conclude that 'She hath a
brave spirit' (l. 140).

Vittoria's suggestion that Monticelso's 'names / Of whore and
murd'ress' proceed from him (ll. 148–9), and her striking metaphor
of spitting into the wind (ll. 150–1), imply that Monticelso's fervour
derives not from a sense of justice, but from his own base desires. It
may be that we see evidence for this in his performance.

152–80   Bracciano finally breaks his silence, which will have been
highly conspicuous by this point: the victimized Vittoria has had no
supporter speak up in her defence since the trial began, despite the
presence of her lover. Even this interjection is hardly indicative of
bravery on Bracciano's part – it might easily be played as a desperate
move by a man who is anxious to make his own alibi heard. Certainly
Bracciano's intervention does nothing to help Vittoria's case, since it
might be interpreted as corroborating Monticelso's allegations of her
lustful behaviour.

The exchange is full of very short, shared lines, as both Bracciano
and Monticelso level accusations at one another: the contrast with
Vittoria's eloquence is strong. Addressing the cardinal as 'Sirrah' – a
term normally used for social inferiors – Bracciano makes a typically violent threat, and as he leaves, he recalls his frosty welcome at
the beginning of the scene by referring to his gown as his 'stool' (l.
172). His parting words, in Latin, warn that 'no one injures me with
impunity' – a threat which allows the audience to anticipate further
bloodshed (l. 179).

Monticelso's observation – 'Your champion's gone' (l. 180) – may
be ironic, since Bracciano hardly behaved as Vittoria's champion
in this scene. Vittoria's response once again highlights the court's

partiality, and continues the play's imagery of its characters as predatory animals.

181–217   Francisco moves the discourse back into a more moderate
tone, and returns to metaphor and insinuation in his attempt to
besmirch Vittoria's reputation: his reference to the use of blood as a
fertiliser (ll. 184V8) is both macabre and foreboding. The tone does
not, however, remain measured for very long. Moving onto the matter
of Vittoria's 'incontinence', Monticelso produces a letter, purportedly
from Bracciano, which supposedly proves their affair. Once again,
he seems to relish the 'lascivious' details just as he refuses to speak
them (ll. 196–8). As Vittoria very reasonably points out, however,
the fact that Bracciano attempted to seduce her does not prove that
she complied. All that she can be convicted of, she concludes, are
'beauty and gay clothes, a merry heart, / And a good stomach to a
feast' (ll. 208–9). Once again, her logic reduces the cardinal to a series
of sarcastic outbursts which are based more on emotion than on
reason. For a third time, Vittoria is likened to a 'devil' in 'good shape'
(ll. 216–17): the description seems increasingly unfair.

218–34   As Francisco demands to know who brought the incriminating letter, Vittoria refuses to answer (l. 220): presumably she is
defending Flamineo (and we may well see this in his reaction). When
Monticelso continues to cite circumstantial evidence against her,
Vittoria insists – quite rightly – that if he will persist in accusing her,
he should step down from his role as judge (ll. 225–6). She suggests
that instead, 'these' should be her 'moderators' (ll. 227–8) – 'these'
referring, of course, to the Ambassadors, but the term is general
enough that it might apply to the audience too. Once again, we are
reminded of our own roles as judges.

235–51   Monticelso's biography of Vittoria does not tally with that
of the historical Vittoria, who was of the Accoramboni family, not
the Vitelli, and born in Gubbio rather than Venice. The fact that
Webster's Vittoria interjects twice suggests that she, too, identifies
inaccuracies in Monticelso's summary of her background, though
presumably these concern the accounts of her sexuality rather
than the details of her birth. His suggestion that her vices 'would

be played a'th'stage' (l. 249) is ironic: for us, of course, they already have been.

252–66   Here, Monticelso turns for the first time in the scene to Flamineo and Marcello: but we should not assume that they have simply sunk into the background over the preceding business. As Vittoria's brothers – and, in Flamineo's case, as an as-yet-undiscovered co-conspirator – their reactions to her trial will have been vital in either building or impeding our sympathy for both her and them. As Monticelso informs them that 'The court hath nothing now to charge you with' (l. 253), we probably see Flamineo breathe a sigh of relief; it may even make us laugh. Certainly he has got off lightly compared with his sister.

Vittoria, meanwhile, is condemned for her 'public' fault (the imputation being that its public nature made it worse than it might have been had it stayed private), and is sentenced to be confined to a 'house of convertites' with her 'bawd'. Flamineo's temporary panic that the word refers to him, and his subsequent relief that it rather refers to Zanche, will probably be comical.

266–94   The actor playing Vittoria will have to decide whether Vittoria's first question here is a sincere one (perhaps she truly does not know what a 'house of convertites' is), or rather a rhetorical strategy aimed at forcing Monticelso to drop his euphemism for something more blunt. Her second question is clearly sarcastic. Francisco's advice that she should 'have patience' implies that she is delivering the lines with some anger, as does the climactic rhythm. When Monticelso observes that she has 'turned Fury' (l. 278), we might remember that Francisco used exactly the same two words to describe Isabella's behaviour at II.i.245 – it seems that legitimate expressions of outrage by women in this world are met almost universally with misogynistic condescension.

Vittoria's anger is understandable. To the Jacobean audience, the 'house of convertites' would probably have summoned immediate connotations of London's own 'house of correction' at Bridewell Prison, where a convicted whore could expect to be whipped publicly. Vittoria's objection that she has been the victim of a 'rape' (l. 274) is a strong metaphor to use – but again, it contains a suggestion that she recognizes Monticelso's behaviour as having been motivated by a sadistic sexuality. When she calls him a 'devil' (l. 280), her words suggest a new contender of the subject of the play's title: Monticelso will, after all, dress in white from IV.iii onwards.

Vittoria uses her final speech to elevate herself above the cardinal, claiming an 'honester' and 'more peaceable' mind. Her final couplet – another *sententia* – builds the speech, and the scene, to a rousing climax. Despite her legal defeat, she has clearly won the moral (and theatrical) victory. It is not unusual for her to exit to applause.

295–301   In the aftermath of this show-stopping moment, Webster splits the stage again between at least two separate conversations. While Monticelso presumably speaks with the Ambassadors upstage, Bracciano re-enters to talk to Francisco. The fact that he has clearly waited until the trial's conclusion to return marks him out as a coward, and his reappearance emphasizes the injustice of the fact that Vittoria has been convicted while the true instigator of the murders, Bracciano himself, has escaped punishment.

Francisco's question, 'Sir, what's the matter?' (l. 298), is an incomplete line of iambic pentameter, suggesting a pause before Bracciano answers. This moment of tension primes the audience to expect imminent news of Isabella's death.

302–8   Flamineo's aside is in prose, suggesting a switch from the elevated verse of the trial to a moment of colloquial complicity with the audience. His cowardly decision to play mad until the trouble has blown over adds a further layer of pretence to the play, and may well make an audience laugh (especially if he starts his 'madman' act immediately).

309–40   Giovanni's entrance with Lodovico signals another sudden contrast in tone: there is nothing remotely funny about a grieving child, and Francisco's reaction to the news of his sister's death is straightforward and understated. The broken and incomplete lines over this exchange suggest a slower, fragmented pace, perhaps with some difficult silences in which no words will suffice. Francisco might find himself unable to offer his nephew any comfort, for example, at lines 326 and 339. Giovanni's naivety and inability to comprehend death poignantly reminds us of the consequences of Vittoria's affair only moments after the scene had (probably) led us to sympathize with her – Webster allows us few straight-cut moral judgements. Francisco's final lines may be both moving and foreboding.

Act III, scene iii

Taking place in a private location outside the courtroom, this scene can, like III.ii, be played as a direct continuation of the previous one (potentially, the whole of Act III could thus be played as one continuous sequence). The first section is often cut in modern performance, but can be a gift for the actor playing Flamineo. The text is gloriously indeterminate: when is he sincere, and when is he merely acting?

1–7 Flamineo enters 'as distracted', feigning madness just as he indicated he would upon his exit in III.ii (l. 309). Pretending to be mad as a means of evading punishment or identification was a stock convention in Renaissance drama: the title character of *Hamlet* and *King Lear*'s Edgar are two famous examples.

The first two lines are noticeably different from what follows: the rhyming couplet reads, perhaps, as a private *sententia* offered in aside to the audience alone, before Flamineo begins his 'performance' of madness in prose which is audible to Marcello and Lodovico. The acting of madness would probably have been recognizable by conventional gestures on the Jacobean stage, but a modern actor will have to decide for himself precisely what form Flamineo's 'madness' takes. Much of his dialogue in this scene is merely a continuation of the kind of cynical, innuendo-laden and metaphorical language we have come to associate with the 'sane' Flamineo anyway, so the extent to which he appears 'mad' will depend to a great extent on the actor's performance choices.

Over lines 3–7, Flamineo expresses his disillusionment in 'service' – like the Conjuror in II.ii, he remains unrewarded by Bracciano for his role in the plot. He expresses his discontent with overblown images of extreme poverty.

8–19 One might wonder whether Flamineo's expressed regret at having served Bracciano is feigned or genuine. Certainly he has cause for resentment, which he will express to Bracciano himself in IV.ii. However, there is a strong sense that his remorse here is for the benefit of the Ambassadors, who enter one-by-one over the next few lines. His performance seems to intensify as his audience grows.

He starts to hint at the way in which Monticelso and Francisco's veneer of respectability hides their true corruption, likening them by implication to 'the devil' (l. 17) – another reference to the play's title.

20–7   Flamineo grows into his performance as once again his audience increases. His musings on the corrupting power of gold might remind the audience of the ways in which minor characters such as Doctor Julio and the Conjurer have already been won over by financial reward in the play. Flamineo turns his ire towards the Lawyer from the previous scene, mocking his pretentious use of the word 'diversivolent' and suggesting a similar corruption: his use of the word 'yon' (l. 23) might suggest that the Lawyer is present or passing (perhaps on his way out of the court). Lines 25–7 make it clear that Flamineo's reflections on corruption refer to Cardinal Monticelso. Once again, the Ambassadors act as a kind of chorus: an onstage audience to whom Flamineo can perform, but with whom he can also interact.

28–34   The chorus is completed by the arrival of the English Ambassador. Flamineo's reference to the English practice of *peine forte et dure* – the pressing to death of prisoners who refused to plead either guilty or not guilty – draws a parallel between the cruelty of Jacobean law and the corruption of the Italian courts. His second allusion to the 'cardinal' (l. 33) makes his allegations of Monticelso's dishonesty even more explicit: a dangerous accusation to make so openly against one so powerful. The Ambassadors' reactions might indicate this.

35–40   Webster's text does not make it clear when the Ambassadors leave the stage, but most modern editors have them exit at line 34. They might, however, stay onstage to witness the whole of the 'strange encounter' (l. 65) which follows. Either way, a director will have to decide exactly to whom Flamineo is performing here, as he controversially denounces religion.

Flamineo continues his diatribe against the corruption which goes unpunished amongst the powerful. His condemnation of 'policy' is somewhat hypocritical, however, since he has described his own

behaviour as 'politic' on two previous occasions (II.i.316 and III.
ii.309). It may be that he is simply acting outrage here.

40–53 Flamineo's vaguely anti-Semitic joke is actually directed at
the corruption of the Church and the nobility. His suggestion that
Marcello will 'swallow all's given thee' (l. 51) reiterates their debate in
III.i (ll. 34–64), implying that his brother is oblivious to the ways in
which his loyalty is regularly exploited by Francisco. The reference to
'Wolner of England' provides another local joke, this time to a famous
glutton of Windsor who would eat anything from iron to glass. As
always, Flamineo is the character in the play most closely tied to
contemporary Jacobean reality – and therefore to the audience.

54–65 In a striking moment of non-mimetic stagecraft, all three
of the scene's characters speak directly to the audience, one after the
other; this stylistic shift is accompanied by a similarly heightened
linguistic transition from prose into verse. The three asides demand
a great deal of physical movement, since Lodovico, Flamineo and
Marcello must each speak to the audience out of one another's
hearing – this is perhaps why Webster indicates Flamineo's exit and
almost immediate re-entrance.

Lodovico divulges that Flamineo has aroused his suspicions,
while Flamineo reveals that he is equally curious about the banished
count's return to Rome. Marcello, meanwhile, simply draws the audience's attention to the fact that the imminent conversation between
Flamineo and Lodovico will be worth 'marking' (l. 65). It is, after all,
the first time that these two characters have met one another, and
they are in many senses parallel: both are cynical outsiders in the
employment of a powerful and corrupt social superior.

66–83 Flamineo curses Lodovico (presumably still in his guise as
a madman); Lodovico replies mock-courteously, though in fact his
response is also a curse (the 'dog-days' were an unpleasantly warm
time of year). Flamineo likens Lodovico to a 'raven' – an evil omen –
before provoking him with a reference to Isabella's death. The provocation is deliberate: Flamineo has indicated already, at lines 60–1, that
he is aware of Lodovico's connection to Isabella.

Recognizing a kindred spirit, perhaps, Lodovico sarcastically
suggests that they should set up house together. Flamineo replies

that they should be 'unsociably sociable' (l. 76), living in discomfort and philosophizing. The shared lines indicate both an energetic pace and a meeting of minds: perhaps their shared joking even implies a begrudging mutual respect. This conversation also marks both characters out as a recognizable stage-type in Renaissance drama: the melancholic. Such characters would complain vehemently about the world, bitter in their impotence to change it, and would frequently be depicted as wishing to retreat into a hermitage or hovel in order to escape it (see, for example, Shakespeare's *Timon of Athens*).

84–97 Most modern editors insert Antonelli and Gasparo's entrance just before the line 'We are observed' (l. 84), but in fact Webster's text does not have Antonelli enter until much later at line 96 (he omits Gasparo's entrance entirely). While Flamineo's indication of 'yon couple' makes sense in reference to Antonelli and Gasparo, then, a director may quite legitimately interpret it as referring to two of the Ambassadors (if they are still onstage), to an imaginary couple (Flamineo is, after all, feigning madness), or even to two members of the audience. Lodovico implies that the 'couple' are 'laughing fools' (l. 85): Antonelli and Gasparo may well be laughing good-naturedly at Lodovico's good fortune, while the Ambassadors may just as easily be laughing with derision at Flamineo and Lodovico's conversation. Interpreted as a reference to the audience, the lines become funny and combative, forging a strong (if somewhat hostile) connection between the characters and the audience.

The theme of melancholy resurfaces in Flamineo's reference to congealed blood (melancholy was supposed to congeal the blood, according to *The Taming of the Shrew*'s Induction 2.128–9). His reference to Fortune's wheel draws upon a popular philosophical metaphor: that an individual's good or bad fortune is at the mercy of the goddess Fortuna, who merely has to turn her wheel in order to raise or lower him. Lodovico set up the image of a capricious Fortune at the beginning of the play (I.i.4–6), and here, Flamineo clearly sees himself at the bottom of her wheel. Implicit in the metaphor, however, is the very dramatic possibility of sudden reversal.

98–110 Fortune's wheel turns immediately – but not for Flamineo. Antonelli brings a signed pardon from the ailing Pope, exonerating

Lodovico of his crimes. Lodovico interrupts his friend's delivery of this news so that he can gloat at the miserable Flamineo.

Flamineo objects to Lodovico's new-found mirth as a betrayal of their melancholic pact. He returns to the motif of a 'great man' or 'politician' who can be privately happy whilst maintaining a public semblance of grief (ll. 107–10). Taken at face value, his words are once again highly hypocritical – presumably we saw Flamineo engaging in precisely this sort of behaviour after Camillo's murder in II.ii's dumb-show.

111–25 This sequence echoes the fast pace of lines 66–83, but now the exchange is openly hostile. Lodovico taunts Flamineo about his sister's disgrace, while Flamineo angrily berates him for his broken promise (though it is possible, of course, that Flamineo is still acting). The argument culminates in a physical scuffle, during which Lodovico attempts to wound Flamineo with his sword (as indicated at line 129). It ends as quickly as it began, as Marcello forces his brother offstage. Lodovico is restrained by Antonelli and Gasparo, in a physical reminder of the play's first scene, and we are left with a sense that this eruption of violence is only a taste of what is in store.

126–36 The final part of this scene is strongly reminiscent of I.i, as Antonelli and Gasparo attempt to pacify a furious Lodovico; the latter's imagery of thunderbolts and earthquakes recalls his earlier talk of 'violent thunder' (I.i.11). The verse in his final speech is somewhat thunder-like itself: punchy, fragmented and threatening imminent danger. His analysis of Flamineo as one of 'These rogues that are most weary of their lives' (l. 130) is perceptive – but might it also apply to Lodovico himself?

Act IV

Act IV, scene i

The play's web of allegiances and counter-allegiances becomes more complicated here, as the cracks in Monticelso and Francisco's alliance start to show. This scene shifts Francisco's role within the play's narrative structure – in one sense, he comes closer to cementing his position as the play's primary antagonist, but in another, he becomes the protagonist of his own revenge tragedy. As his role shifts, so will the audience's sympathies.

1–11 We see immediately that Francisco is keeping his thoughts secret from Monticelso. The cardinal appears to be trying to provoke Francisco into taking revenge on Bracciano, while Francisco seems to resist, pointing out that punishments for the sins committed by soldiers during a war will be inflicted in the afterlife upon the head of state who caused the war. In performance, his answer may seem convincing – we will learn shortly, however, that it is a 'political' one. Monticelso's metaphor of a virgin bride's hair once again seems inappropriately sexual for a cleric.

12–27 Francisco maintains that he is uninterested in revenge. However, Monticelso's images of sleeping revenge, waiting to erupt, add to the scene's sense of tension, and build on similar effects established earlier in the play. The references to the 'thunder yonder' (l. 23) and 'the cannon' (l. 14) recall Francisco and Bracciano's argument in II.i, when the same images were used twice each (ll. 61–3, 72–3), and of course the anticipation of impending 'thunder' has become a recurring motif (see also I.i.11 and III.iii.128). These references have a strong cumulative effect.

28–37 Francisco changes the subject, apparently casually – but it might be clear to the audience that the 'black book' of Monticelso's which he requests to see is the first stage in a solo revenge plan which he intends to pursue without the cardinal's help. The 'black book' contains Monticelso's list of the city's wrongdoers, and has been put together with the help of 'intelligence' (l. 30) – in other words, spies and informers. When we see this book, its size will indicate just how corrupt the world of the play is: not only the number of criminals which inhabit it, but also the extent of its duplicity and espionage (there is an opportunity for humour here – the book could be enormous). The imagery of 'conjuring' and 'devils' (ll. 35–6) once again associate Monticelso with unholy, unwholesome activities, and when he returns, the image of a red-robed Cardinal holding a big black book might even appear devilish.

37–42   This is Francisco's first soliloquy in the play, and is Webster's first step in transforming Francisco into a protagonist of sorts. Though he had no soliloquies at all over the first seven scenes of the play, he will have several over the remaining nine. Apostrophizing Monticelso (it is significant that he does not address the audience directly straight away), Francisco reveals that he does not trust the cardinal, and that he plans to act alone.

43–76   As Monticelso presents his book, the verse breaks into fragmentary lines – this probably indicates that he is reading as he speaks. The criminals in Monticelso's book are largely swindlers and conmen of various sorts, and their crimes are generally ones of cunning and duplicity rather than violence. The theme, once again, is deceptive appearances; this is ironic, since Francisco himself is making a pretence of his honesty before our eyes.

Francisco interrupts Monticelso as he sees the page where the city's murderers are listed, and requests to borrow the book. Though he affects an interest in justice, it will be clear to the audience that his true motivations are less honourable.

77–97   Left alone, Francisco begins what will be the play's longest soliloquy – a remarkable turnaround for a character whose thoughts and motives have until now been largely unavailable to the audience. This development may come as something of a surprise to an audience who have been expecting to follow Vittoria and Flamineo as their protagonists, and it suggests that even the play's villains are not to be taken at face value.

Francisco explains his interpretation of Monticelso's book: that the cardinal and his officers use it to blackmail the city's criminals, rather than to bring them to justice. He resolves to make just as corrupt a use of it, as a catalogue in which he can seek out murderous accomplices. His rhyming *sententia* at lines 96–7 makes much the same point about religion as Flamineo did in the previous scene (III. iii.38–40).

98–115   This is the second of the three supernatural apparition sequences which are almost equally spaced throughout the play (if we count the dumb-shows in II.ii as one rather than two). Like the one which will follow in V.iv, this is the arrival of a silent ghost, whose appearance is framed by a long soliloquy from the person to whom the ghost appears. Like the Conjurer who summoned the dumb-shows in II.ii, Francisco appears to be in control of the apparition here, both summoning its entrance and demanding its departure. Unusually for plays of this period – in which the appearance of ghosts was highly conventional – Isabella's ghost is presented relatively unambiguously as the product of Francisco's melancholy imagination.

The appearance of the ghost does, of course, present all sorts of questions for the performer, for the director and for the designer. How is Isabella dressed? How does she move? Where on the stage does she stand, and how far away is she from Francisco? Does she take an upstage position, forcing Francisco downstage towards the audience? (Presumably she would have done at the Red Bull, where the entrances to the stage would have been at the back.) Or is there an interesting tension as Francisco moves incredulously around her? How does he 'remove' her? By closing his eyes, perhaps, or turning away? Is this done violently or sadly?

The theatrical effect will be pronounced: not only will the audience be taken aback by the appearance of the ghost, but they may also be surprised by Francisco's various reactions. The sequence may well build sympathy for a previously unsympathetic character.

115–30 Francisco's dismissal of his sister's ghost marks his transition from heartfelt grief to heartless revenge, and this reversal may well be illustrated physically. His resolution to revenge marks him out – somewhat belatedly – as a conventional figure in Jacobean drama: the hero of a revenge tragedy. This is confirmed by his own description of his plot as 'My tragedy' (l. 119). Other examples of the genre include *The Spanish Tragedy*, *The Revenger's Tragedy*, *Hamlet* and to an extent Webster's own *The Duchess of Malfi*; the appearance of a ghost was often the catalyst for the hero's action, and the hero would usually operate (as Francisco will) by cunning and disguise.

One might wonder, though, whether Francisco is appealing enough as a character to become a true protagonist. He begins his 'tragedy' with an ugly relish, promising to find 'some idle mirth' in pretending to be in love with Vittoria (l. 119). He writes a love letter to her, presumably very quickly, before congratulating himself and summoning a servant to deliver it to Vittoria at the house of convertites 'when some followers / Of Bracciano may be by' (ll. 129–30). His scheming is becoming truly Machiavellian.

131–9   Francisco's final soliloquy of the scene informs us that he has picked Lodovico as his assassin – though presumably he did not need the 'black book' for this, since he has already sought Lodovico's pardon from the dying Pope (III.iii.92–4). His resolution to procure the count's services with 'gold' recalls Flamineo's lamentation at III. iii.21–7, while the bloodlust he exhibits as he leaves, and his parting line (a motto in Latin which reveals his own 'devilish' allegiances), suggest that he may still be more villain than hero. An actor will find it difficult to make Francisco sympathetic over these lines; it may be, however, that the sequence with Isabella's ghost has already done precisely this.

Act IV, scene ii

In the kind of fluid dramaturgy typical of the Jacobean playhouse's open stage, this scene takes place ambiguously both inside the house of convertites and outside it. At the beginning of the scene, the various exchanges are clearly taking place at the entrance, but the stage direction at line 128 – '*She throws herself upon a bed*' – makes it clear that by this point a transition to an indoor location has taken place. How the bed makes its way onto the stage is not clear, but it is likely that the scene made some use of the discovery space (much like the dumb-shows in II.ii). However it appears, the visual impact of an onstage bed is important for the scene, concerned as it is with the nuances of a private and tempestuous sexual relationship.

Dramatically, this scene provides another important reversal: it is Vittoria's lowest moment before her ascent in Act V, but after a series of arguments with Bracciano, the lovers are reunited and make their escape. The frantic stage business with the letter, multiple arguments and ever-shifting allegiances between the three main characters create a hurtling pace; Flamineo's imagery of whirlpools and whirlwinds might be understood as metaphors for the scene itself (ll. 71, 106).

1–6   The matron of the house of convertites expresses her concern that she will be punished for allowing Bracciano access to Vittoria;

Flamineo assures her that the authorities are far too concerned with the impending death of the Pope to worry about the 'guarding of a lady' (l. 6). In fact, the matron's concerns are justified: just moments after the announcement of the new Pope in the next scene, Francisco will order the matron's arrest (IV.iii.50–1). One might wonder what has persuaded her to take the risk. Certainly it would not be out of keeping with the play's themes for her to have been bribed, and we may well see some evidence of this.

7–21　Francisco's servant enters only moments after his departure from the previous scene: clearly the plot is picking up pace. He delivers the letter as instructed, and in so doing arouses Bracciano's suspicions – just as Francisco had intended. The swiftness with which the letter changes hands here is striking: within just seven lines (most of them shared between more than one speaker), it has passed from the servant, to the matron, to Flamineo, to Bracciano (ll. 10–16). Bracciano enters just as the servant leaves – perhaps they pass one another – and within two lines, the matron has exited into the house of convertites. Everything about the stagecraft of this scene informs the audience that the letter is a vital prop which will cause a whirl-wind of problems.

22–40　His jealousy aroused by the inscription on the outside of the letter, Bracciano resolves to tear it open 'were't her heart' (l. 22). The image does not suggest that he is likely to respond lightly to the contents. Determining that it has come from Francisco ('Florence'), he accuses Vittoria of 'juggling' – two-timing him – before demanding that Flamineo read the letter aloud (ll. 23–4). The audience will watch, then, as Bracciano gets angrier and angrier in silence, while a presumably nervous Flamineo attempts to make light of the letter as he reads it. Played well, the sequence will be both funny and unsettling: each time Flamineo breaks away from the increasingly inflammatory letter to make a quip, something about his employer's non-verbal response forces him to return to his reading. The letter itself is written in rather stilted language, and Flamineo (and audiences) might be amused by its forced rhymes.

41–61　Bracciano's response to the letter is, inevitably, an explosion of anger; it is notable that this anger is directed entirely at Vittoria and not at the letter's author. Clearly Bracciano reads the letter as evidence of her infidelity, but as Vittoria herself pointed out in relation to another incriminating letter at her trial, the fact that a letter has been written to her proves nothing (III.ii.192–206). In calling his lover a 'whore', Bracciano uses precisely the same term as her accusers in III.ii – and now that we are party to Francisco's plot, it seems even more unfair.

Flamineo defends his sister, and defies his employer for the first time. Bracciano's line 'Do you brave? Do you stand me?' implies a literal stand-off (l. 51), while 'Would you be kicked?' also suggests physical proximity. Flamineo's response – 'Would you have your neck broke?' – not only matches Bracciano's threat with a stronger one, but also reminds him of the manner in which Flamineo murdered Camillo (l. 54). Flamineo's short speech about 'degrees of evils' and 'degrees of devils' is outspoken and courageous, suggesting as it does that Bracciano is more evil than Flamineo because of his greater power (ll. 58–60).

62–71 Flamineo's insubordination seems to force Bracciano to back down; the Duke attempts to downgrade his servant's defiance to mere 'prating' (l. 62). Flamineo observes, with characteristic wit, that the Duke's kindness to him has been nothing more than an absence of violence (ll. 63–6), and promises to lead him into the house of convertites. Their exchange at lines 68–71 suggests that Flamineo walks backwards, staring his employer in the face as he does so: a physical illustration of their lack of trust.

72–83 Vittoria enters, and the scene transforms from outside the house of convertites to inside it. The open stage of Jacobean playhouses could accommodate such indeterminacy (III.v of *Romeo and Juliet* is similarly both inside and outside the house), requiring the audience simply to imagine a change of location. The scene change is accomplished primarily through the use of language: in this respect, it allows a fluid use of space more akin to modern film than naturalistic theatre. Alternatively, Vittoria (and her bed) might have been revealed in the discovery space if Flamineo drew the curtain on line 71.

The question of whether Vittoria comes to Bracciano and Flamineo, or whether they intrude upon her, is an important one for the dynamics of this scene. If she arrives suddenly and unannounced, then she has the upper hand at the beginning of their conversation; if, on the other hand, she is discovered in her bedroom, then Bracciano enters already on the attack. Presumably wherever she is, she is upstage and fairly central: a position of relative power.

Bracciano's dialogue here is angry and combative, but Vittoria responds calmly (though perhaps with some incredulity). The letter changes hands once again, necessitating some physical contact between the lovers; Bracciano's desire to see Vittoria's 'cabinet' presumably entails some sort of movement towards the exit, which is stopped by Vittoria's reply. Flamineo probably occupies a peripheral position at the edge of the stage, from where he delivers his cryptic warning to Bracciano to 'Ware hawk' (l. 83).

84–102 Vittoria reads the letter and identifies it as a 'treacherous plot' (l. 84), but Bracciano seems more willing to believe that she has been unfaithful. His diatribe here is rhetorical, with much of it directed at Vittoria herself, but a great deal is addressed elsewhere. The line 'How long have I beheld the devil in crystal?' (l. 88) – another reference to Vittoria as a 'white devil' – is probably not directed at either of the other characters present, while lines 99–100 are clearly apostrophized to Isabella, Bracciano's 'sweetest duchess'. The actor playing Bracciano may even appeal to the audience in his condemnation of Vittoria, recalling the judgemental role they were asked to play in her trial scene: he might easily gesture outwards as he asserts that 'all the world speaks ill' of her (l. 102). Bracciano's lines here require a physical performance which is as 'scattered' as the thoughts he accuses Vittoria of having, and his metaphor of himself and his lover as 'two adamants' (magnets) shunning one another might provide the basis for further physicalization (ll. 93–4). The sequence is energetic and chaotic.

102–6 Bracciano's invocation of Isabella's memory clearly enrages Vittoria, who responds here with a dignified anger. In keeping with Bracciano's suggestion that they should be like 'two adamants', she meets his accusations with an equal and opposite force. This is illustrated most neatly in lines 105–6, as she completes the second half of his line 'Whose death God pardon' by twisting his own words back upon him: 'Whose death God revenge / On thee, most godless duke'.

The force with which she speaks this curse may be what silences Bracciano, who does not speak again for another 23 lines.

Flamineo's aside is spoken from the periphery again, probably directly to the audience, who may even laugh. The image of the lovers as 'two whirlwinds' is another strikingly physical one, which may well find its way into the scene's choreography: Vittoria and Bracciano probably move violently and passionately, and might circle around each other, making full use of the stage space.

107–28 Vittoria silences Bracciano with a long and powerful speech, which results in his capitulation and remorse. She points out what the dramaturgy of III.ii seemed calculated to make the audience notice: that she has suffered 'infamy' while he got away scot-free (l. 107). 'What do you call this house?' (l. 113) must be accompanied by a physical gesture, either towards the fictive space of the tiring house or (more likely) the playhouse itself; if the latter, then the audience are once again implicated in the scene's debate. Her speech, like Bracciano's, implies a dynamic use of space. She asks a series of rhetorical questions of both Bracciano and the audience (ll. 113–18), orders him to leave the space (ll. 118–20), and envisages her own wounded ascent to heaven (ll. 122–3) before retreating to her bed and throwing herself upon it. She commands, and then willingly relinquishes, the stage.

129–35 Moved by the force of her speech, Bracciano resumes his former loving attitude towards Vittoria. His question 'Why do you weep?' (l. 131) is either disingenuous or stupid, since the cause of her distress is frankly obvious, having been eloquently articulated only moments earlier. Bracciano's affection takes a rather disturbingly possessive tone as he describes the resistant Vittoria's eyes and lips as 'mine' (ll. 133–4). He probably touches her face as she shrugs him off.

136–48 Flamineo – who has been uncharacteristically quiet over this – interjects to suggest that Vittoria should forgive Bracciano. It may be that he suspects her of making a show of grief in order to gain the upper hand, and is concerned that she may be pushing it too far. She responds angrily, using the same term to insult him as Bracciano used earlier on – he is a 'pandar' (l. 136). Bracciano attempts to excuse his jealous behaviour, but she rejects him contemptuously. Again, the push-and-pull of this scene can be strongly physicalized.

149–62 Flamineo's attempt to reconcile the lovers is typically duplicitous, as he says one thing to Bracciano, another to Vittoria, and something else entirely to the audience. Webster's text does not make it clear which lines are asides and which are spoken aloud, so it is up to the modern editor (and the actor) to interpret the speech. Flamineo's misogynistic insults might seem more suited to asides, but it would not be unusual for him to air offensive opinions aloud; this would also be in keeping with his new-found outspokenness to Bracciano. On the other hand, there is enormous comic potential in having Flamineo scuttle from one character to the other, quipping conspiratorially to the audience as he does so. Another variation has him muttering asides to Bracciano out of Vittoria's hearing, and then speaking loudly so that she hears only what he wants her to. This would be reminiscent of his conversation with her at I.ii.123–44, in which they duped Camillo, and might hint at a reversal in their relationship: whereas in Act I she was the privileged party in this game, now she is the excluded one.

163–98 As Bracciano takes up the task of winning Vittoria back, Flamineo continues to offer advice, becoming increasingly (and perhaps comically) superfluous to his master's efforts. Both Vittoria and Bracciano ignore him. Perhaps in response to this, Flamineo then digresses into some highly misogynistic observations (ll. 181–5) which are either cynical asides to the audience, or inflammatory statements designed to undermine Bracciano's amorous advances. Vittoria's complaint about Bracciano's treatment of her at lines 192–3 is trenchant, and she keeps her promise to 'speak not one word more' for the rest of the scene. On the page, it is easy to underestimate the dramatic power of a defiantly silent character on stage in such an intimate scene; in performance, it will be clear to the audience that all is not as 'well' as Flamineo suggests (l. 198). His metaphor of a turning tide, however, suggests that the 'whirlpool' has been calmed to an extent.

199–223 Flamineo suggests that Bracciano and Vittoria should sleep together in silence, as the Greeks must have done while they hid in the Trojan horse (ll. 201–2). The image is surprising and striking, suggesting that their affair remains illicit, dangerous and somewhat squalid. Bracciano changes the subject, and both he and Flamineo complain about their treatment in Rome. They hatch a plan to escape to Padua with Vittoria, the rest of her family and Giovanni, and Bracciano promises both her and Flamineo advancement. Quite how Vittoria reacts to all this is unclear: she remains silent, and it is up to the actor to decide whether this is down to stubbornness, anger, resentment, or something else.

224–49   This last section of the scene brings a sudden shift in tone. Bracciano's plan had invested the scene with a sense of momentum, but this is now interrupted as Flamineo starts to relate a long allegory, for reasons which are not immediately obvious. Webster certainly borrowed this fable (probably from Edward Topsell's *History of Serpents*, 1608), and his audience may have been familiar with it themselves. Bracciano's interpretation is the obvious one, particularly given Flamineo's complaint earlier in this scene that his master had left him 'to be devoured last' (ll. 63–5). Flamineo appears to be warning him, threatening violent reprisal if Bracciano breaks his promise of courtly reward; the two characters may stand off against each other for a moment as they did earlier in the scene. Flamineo promptly backs away from this implication, though, suggesting a less offensive but much less plausible interpretation (which he himself admits does not hold 'in every particle').

His final aside reveals that he is fully aware of the dangerous game he is playing with his 'varying of shapes'. Its imagery echoes the concluding speech of I.ii, in which he promised to imitate 'The subtle foldings of a winter's snake' on his route to power (I.ii.353). This echo serves to remind the audience that Flamineo is still busy putting into practice the plan for self-promotion he has had since the very beginning of the play.

Act IV, scene iii

In contrast with the previous scene's intimacy, this scene utilizes costume, spectacle and every part of the stage space in order to maximize its visual impact. Its public spectacle is twice disrupted by intrusions from the private: the servant enters with news of Vittoria's escape amidst the ceremony of the announcement of the new Pope, and Francisco breaks the news to Monticelso just seconds after the latter's first appearance, in state, in his new public role. The second image especially provides a strong visual illustration of corrupt and underhand political manoeuvring.

At just over three-fifths of the way through the play, as Vittoria, Flamineo and Bracciano's fortunes are on the rise, but as the revenge plot against them is also under way, the end of this scene is a good place for an interval (Act V is much longer than any of the other four).

1–17   The stage set-up is complex here. Lodovico and Gasparo are guarding the entrance to the conclave – a sealed-off holy space in which the cardinals are now meeting to elect the new Pope. In this scene, the conclave is located just offstage, so the onstage door which leads to it will be invested with a huge amount of spatial importance. The Ambassadors exit from it and onto the stage; it may be that they enter one-by-one as they are described by Lodovico over lines 5–14. There would have been two doors onto the Red Bull's stage, one each side of the tiring house: Lodovico and Gasparo guard one, while Francisco enters at the other. Francisco has not entered the conclave, but his words indicate that he is taking charge of the proceedings' security. Perhaps the Ambassadors greet him in the middle of the stage, while Lodovico and Gasparo provide a commentary from the edge.

The Ambassadors are dressed in the magnificent outfits of particular knightly orders. Visual spectacle and pageantry were important to Jacobean audiences: they lived in a society where their most direct encounters with those in authority tended to be through visual displays of power. Nowhere was this more immediately noticeable than in costume, which was highly codified: until 1604, dress had been regulated by the 'sumptuary laws', which permitted only men and women of a certain social rank to wear particular types of clothing. At the theatre, of course, where scenery was minimal, actors relied upon eye-catching costumes not only as signifiers of power and social status, but also for powerful visual effect.

17–34   Francisco's question implies that he has lost sight of Lodovico (with whom he has already spoken at lines 1–3), so the stage must be awash with activity. He orders Lodovico to 'marshal' the cardinals' food, which arrives – in another rich visual display, perhaps – in covered dishes. The French and English Ambassadors once again act as a chorus (see also III.ii.106–7, III.ii.140, and III.iii.8–34), interpreting the action for the audience. The very act of searching the dishes smacks of the potential for – and suspicion of – corruption amongst the high-ranking clergy.

35–46 Webster makes good use here of the windows and balcony which overlooked the stage at the Red Bull. A Conclavist looks down from the window, alerting the party below to the fact that the announcement of the new Pope is imminent. The Cardinal of Arragon then appears on the balcony to announce, in Latin, that Monticelso has been elected Pope. The balcony would have been the most authoritative position on the stage: central, elevated and probably rather splendidly decorated. When the Cardinal speaks, then, everything about him signifies religious authority: his stage position, his costume, his props (he probably holds a cross in his hands) and his language.

47–58 In true Websterian style, the stage is spilt once again between the official and the unofficial, the public and the (semi-) private. A servant (possibly the same servant who conveyed the letter in III.i. and III.ii) hurries onto the lower part of the stage and shares a rushed exchange with Francisco about Vittoria's escape; this plays out against the magnificent backdrop of the Cardinal and the Ambassadors in all their official regalia. Francisco makes a show of outrage (presumably for the benefit of these officials) before confiding to the audience that he is secretly pleased by this development.

59–70 Webster gives no description of the ceremony surrounding Monticelso's first entrance as Pope other than that he enters 'in state'. There must be a strong visual sense of Monticelso's new-found authority: he is probably surrounded by church officials, and it may be that he is carried in on a great chair. In a conspicuous change from his previous (and much commented-upon) red robes of a Cardinal, he is now almost certainly wearing white. The costume change will suggest the parallel change in Monticelso's character which this scene will go on to demonstrate; it may also link him, once again, to the title of the play.

His first pronouncement as Pope, in Latin, is to forgive the sins of the assembled party. Upon hearing of Vittoria's escape from Francisco, however, he then rather incongruously excommunicates both her and Bracciano and 'all that are theirs in Rome' (l. 69). The actual act of excommunication would involve the ringing of a bell, the closing of a Bible and the extinguishing of a candle, so it is probable that Monticelso merely resolves to perform the rite here rather than acting it out in full. He then leaves the stage, taking all its pageantry with him.

71–9   The mass exodus transforms the stage once again into a private space. Francisco reminds Lodovico that he has 'ta'en the sacrament' to kill Bracciano (l. 72) – an odd phrase, since murder is explicitly condemned by the Bible, but one which serves to remind the audience of the many hypocrisies of the outwardly 'moral' characters in this play. Francisco makes it clear that despite his high social status, he intends to share in the 'glory' of the murder himself (l. 79). He leaves in a hurry, as Monticelso re-enters: the latter's words at lines 90–2 indicate that Francisco bows to Lodovico as he leaves. Though the stage direction in the text reads 'exit', it makes more sense for Francisco to remain on stage, or return to the stage, and observe Lodovico's conversation with Monticelso, unseen by both: his anticipation of Lodovico's change of heart at the end of the scene is otherwise difficult to explain.

80–96   Monticelso re-enters, alone. The contrast with his previous appearance, only lines earlier, will be marked – this is Monticelso in his private, unofficial identity, as opposed to his new public one as Pope. Francisco's sudden exit probably arouses Monticelso's suspicions, and he questions Lodovico as to the nature of his connection with Francisco. Lodovico replies enigmatically.

97–116   Accustomed to being in a position of knowledge, Monticelso is angered by Lodovico's evasions, and demands to know the truth. Rather surprisingly, Lodovico suddenly agrees to tell him, noting 'I care not greatly if I do' (l. 105): but he prefaces his disclosure by making it clear to Monticelso that he speaks it as a confession to a priest, obliging Monticelso never to reveal it. Monticelso's response – 'You have o'erta'en me' (l. 110) – indicates that he has been outwitted. Unless this is merely a strategy to loosen Lodovico's tongue, this is a different Monticelso from the cunning arch-manipulator we saw earlier.

116–27   In his last speech, Monticelso surprises us once again. Where only two scenes earlier he appeared to be urging revenge (III.i.12–21), he now condemns Lodovico (and, by implication, Francisco) for their planned murder, warning that no good can come of such violence. As he leaves, he warns Lodovico that he must repent, likening his evil to a 'cruel devil' (l. 127). The audience might wonder what has happened to Monticelso: Has his new holy office purified his thoughts? Is he condemning the revenge plot because he is morally obliged to do so, or simply because he has been excluded from it by his former co-conspirator? Is he speaking here as Pope rather than as Monticelso, thinking one thing in secret but saying another? These questions remain unresolved as he leaves the stage for the last time.

128–53   Shaken by the Pope's condemnation, Lodovico decides to give up the revenge plot. Francisco, however – having either observed or anticipated this twist – skilfully manipulates the count back towards his own plans. He immediately sends a thousand crowns to Lodovico, instructing his servant to tell him they are from the Pope. Upon receiving them, Lodovico interprets the gift as a secret endorsement of the planned murder from the Pope himself. He speaks appreciatively of 'the art, / The modest form of greatness' (ll. 143–4), admiring Monticelso's 'cunning' (l. 149) in appearing to disapprove whilst secretly approving: his metaphor once again suggests an undercurrent of lust beneath Monticelso's frosty exterior. Ironically, Lodovico's praise applies to Francisco rather than to the Pope – the Duke having been so 'cunning' that even his accomplices fail to recognize it.

Act V

Act V, scene i

Everything about this scene seems calculated to wrong-foot the audience: new characters, a new location, disguises and unexpected developments in character relationships. Like the previous one, it is busy, full of exits and entrances, and in its opening procession, potentially spectacular. Once again, we witness characters switching suddenly from public to private behaviour, and *vice versa*.

There is also another, more sophisticated link between this scene and the last. IV.iii concluded with a soliloquy in which Lodovico compared what he perceived as Monticelso's Machiavellian scheming with the behaviour of 'brides at wedding dinners', who sit, he says,

> with their looks turned
> From the least wanton jests, their puling stomach
> Sick of the modesty, when their thoughts are loose,
> Even acting of those hot and lustful sports
> Are to ensue about midnight. (IV.iii.144–9)

Now, mere seconds later, Webster presents us with the actual image of a bride at a wedding feast. The same Ambassadors who attended Monticelso's election as Pope are present, and a similar procession takes place. Just as in the trial scene, the ostensibly opposite Vittoria and Monticelso are made parallel to one another.

This is also the first appearance of 'Mulinassar', the persona adopted by the disguised Francisco. The text makes it clear that Mulinassar is a 'Moor' – a North African, like both Zanche and the non-speaking character 'Little Jaques the Moor' (who is mentioned in a Quarto stage direction in II.i). In modern performances, the fact that Francisco, usually played by a white actor, is required to disguise himself as a character of a different ethnicity can be a sensitive and problematic issue: regardless of the fact that it is difficult to make the disguise at all convincing, 'blacking up' has become increasingly taboo in recent years. Philip Prowse's 1991 production for the National Theatre solved the issue by putting Francisco in a lavish turban with a triangular covering to obscure his face, while Philip Franks's staging for the Lyric Hammersmith in 2000 costumed him as a Palestinian militiaman in a headscarf.

s.d. This '*passage over the stage*' recalls similar processions at the beginnings of scenes I.ii and III.ii (and those in the previous scene). It is almost certainly Bracciano and Vittoria's wedding procession. It marks a change of status for many of the characters depicted: Vittoria has transformed from a disgraced woman to an exalted figure, while both she and Bracciano – recently excommunicated by the Pope himself – are central and powerful here. Cornelia and Marcello have evidently overcome their objections to Bracciano enough that they are willing to be his guests. Lines 57–61 suggest that the Ambassadors should be part of this procession, too: an ironic turn of events, since they witnessed the couple's excommunication. The sequence might thus be read as a wordless commentary on the amorality and shifting allegiances of power.

1–3   This public scene gives way immediately to a private one. Flamineo evidently believes that he has shared in his sister's turnaround in fortune; this confidence is reflected in his use of verse rather than his usual prose. His new-found status might be visible in the staging – Flamineo might wear a new costume, perhaps, or be attended by servants. Alternatively, the absence of any visible change in Flamineo's status might suggest to an audience that the character's expectation of reward remains unlikely to be fulfilled. He remains onstage after the rest of the procession leaves, after all, which suggests that he is still a marginal figure in the world of the court. A director's decision regarding the status of Hortensio (which is unclear) will have a significant impact upon our interpretation of Flamineo's status here, too: if Flamineo is chatting with a courtier, then his assertion of happiness might be taken at face value; if, on the other hand, Hortensio is a lowly servant, we might suspect Flamineo of self-deception.

4–43   This long passage introduces us to what will seem to us at first to be three new, as-yet-unseen characters: Mulinassar the Moor, and the two Capuchin monks who keep him company. Though we will shortly discover that these characters are Francisco, Lodovico and Gasparo in disguise, the play so far has given the audience no intimation of this plot. We may, of course, be suspicious of the introduction of so many new characters at such a late point in the play – and we certainly know that a revenge plot of some sort is under way – but evidently Flamineo suspects nothing. This marks another reversal for this character, who has previously been largely in control or at least in full knowledge of the various subterfuges. Flamineo's observation about glow worms is ironic, since he is unaware that the soldier to whom his lines refer is the disguised Francisco.

44–62 Having aroused our curiosity about 'Mulinassar', Webster brings him onto the stage. Whether or not an audience will recognize him immediately as the disguised Francisco will depend on the production: it was common in Webster's day (as it is now) for actors to double, and (unlike in modern performance) black characters would have been played by white actors in make-up anyway. The two silent, hooded monks (Capuchins wore long, pointed hoods) are likely to arouse the audience's suspicion, since their identities are hidden; 'Mulinassar's' identity may also be hinted at, therefore, by association. It is possible, of course, that the identities of all three characters will be abundantly clear to the audience, and a production may legitimately rely merely upon theatrical convention to convince us that the other characters are taken in by the disguises. In such a case, the scene has a darkly comic potential.

Most editors add an entrance for Carlo and Pedro here, since these characters speak at lines 63–7. Presumably they are members of Bracciano's court who have been bribed to betray him from 'the inside' – Francisco hinted that he had such spies within Bracciano's court at IV.iii.76–7. This would mean that of the nine characters onstage alongside Bracciano at this point, no less than six are secretly preparing to betray him (possibly seven, if the undeveloped character named as 'Farnese' in the Quarto stage direction is a conspirator).

63–85 This betrayal becomes evident as soon as Bracciano, Flamineo and Hortensio leave the stage, and Carlo and Pedro welcome Francisco (and probably the other conspirators) to the court. Presumably Lodovico and Gasparo throw back their hoods to reveal their identities. It may be that in the name of theatrical clarity, Francisco also removes some part of his disguise: high-status Moors on the Jacobean stage would probably have worn white turbans, like those depicted in the woodcut of a 'Moor' in Cesare Vecellio's *Habiti Antichi* (1590) and in a contemporary portrait of Abd el-Ouahed ben Messaoud, the Moorish Ambassador to Queen Elizabeth I (c. 1600).

This private conversation will probably be whispered and hurried, since the conspirators are in danger of being overheard and discovered at any moment. It is ironic that Carlo and Pedro have 'sealed' their vows 'with the sacrament' (l. 64), since their actions are distinctly unholy. This underscores the confusion of religious faith and violence which was manifest in Flamineo's speech at lines

13–23, and which is illustrated visually by the murderers' disguises as monks. Their conversation makes it clear that an attempt to murder Bracciano is imminent, but the audience are left guessing as to the method. Before we can learn, the conspirators are interrupted by Flamineo's re-entrance, and they hurriedly vacate the stage.

86–96   This short passage is the first in the play to establish Zanche as a character with a storyline of her own. She is bound to have aroused the audience's curiosity, having been visually conspicuous throughout as the main black character on stage. She has been almost silent until now, speaking only once (at I.ii.214). Now, her role in the play starts to become clear: she has begun some kind of romantic relationship with Flamineo, of which Marcello clearly disapproves. Whether his disapproval stems from Zanche's association with the disgraced Vittoria, or from his own racist attitude towards her ethnicity, is up to the actor – his reference to her as a 'devil' (commonly associated with blackness in the Jacobean period) may suggest the latter.

Flamineo's lines suggest that he is physically aroused by her presence, so the two of them may be engaged in some sort of sexual contact as they enter the stage – perhaps she 'sticks' to him physically, as suggested in line 93. She is quickly distracted, however, by the presence of Mulinassar, her 'countryman' (l. 94). We see later that she has formed an instant attraction to him (ll. 214–17), and it may be that we see some evidence for this here. She leaves the stage suddenly – this might have something to do with Marcello's hostile body language.

97–121   Francisco uses his persona as 'Mulinassar' to forge a connection with Flamineo and Marcello. It is significant that he uses prose, traditionally reserved for straight-talking characters, to create the illusion of a down-to-earth character, when of course he is anything but.

The whole passage is steeped in irony. 'Mulinassar' gives voice to seemingly progressive (even subversive) ideas about the way in which he and the Duke are 'all made of one clay' and suggests that social rank is simply a matter of 'chance': the speaker, though, is himself a Duke, and the audience's knowledge of this undermines the egalitarian principles to which he appears to be giving expression. (A further level of complexity is added to this, however, when one considers that this is a performance-within-a-performance – the Duke who is playing Mulinassar is himself being played by a lowly actor.) Mulinassar condemns those men who 'seem Colossuses in a chamber, who, if they came into the field, would appear pitiful pigmies' (ll. 120–1), when of course Francisco (and the actor who speaks these lines) is also merely pretending to be a great soldier.

122–42 Flamineo boasts that his Machiavellian (even cowardly) approach towards courtly advancement allows him some safety; in yet another bird metaphor, Francisco compares him to a pigeon who may not be shot because he belongs 'to the lord of the manor' (l. 130). The metaphor has a rather menacing implication: such pigeons are, of course, bred only so that they can be killed for the lord's consumption at a later date. The audience will be aware that Flamineo's perception of his own safety is already inaccurate simply because he is unaware of the disguised Francisco's true identity. This puts the audience in an interesting position: we are now aware of crucial plot information, while the character to whom we have thus far been closest is not. Do we enjoy this reversal in Flamineo's level of control and awareness, or do we pity him?

143–61 The subject of Hortensio's question at line 145 – 'What's he?' – is unclear. Does his question refer to Francisco, or to the 'young lord' who has just spoken? Either way, Flamineo's answer indicates that they are discussing somebody who is playing the court game and advancing himself by flattery and deception.

Flamineo and Hortensio clearly speak to one another in secret here, probably positioning themselves downstage while the other characters set up the 'barriers' for V.iii behind them. This proximity to the audience invites us into their confidence. Flamineo calls Hortensio his 'sworn brother' (l. 152), implying a contrast with his actual brother, Marcello: whereas he is secretive and riddling with Marcello, he tells Hortensio the truth. He reveals that all that is keeping him close to Zanche is her knowledge of his 'villainy' (l. 154). His image of woman as a 'wolf' recalls Bracciano's description of Vittoria at IV.ii.92.

162–85 Flamineo's duplicity is once again the focus of the play's comedy, as his furtive conversation about Zanche is interrupted by

Zanche herself; he greets her with a two-faced pretence of fond-
ness. Zanche accuses him of losing interest in her sexually, while
Flamineo responds in riddles – his insincerity is manifest. There is
a strong suggestion that Flamineo may have persuaded Zanche to
consummate their relationship by promising that he would marry
her – a promise which, if he did make it, he evidently has no intention of keeping. We might get a greater sense of this subtext in
performance.

186–213   Cornelia's sudden entrance and equally swift exit marks
another change in pace for this scene; it also moves the scene back
into verse. Her interruption might remind the audience of her intrusion into I.ii at line 270. Though she and her son Marcello have previously been associated with an honourable, straightforward morality
(see I.ii.272–316 and III.i.32–63 respectively), they both display a
vicious hatred towards Zanche here. The play's absence of stable
ethical reference points is an indication of its moral complexity.

This unanticipated flash of violence may well surprise an audience (and will probably build sympathy for its victim). Flamineo's
outraged response may also work to his favour in the audience's
estimation of him. His argument with Marcello is fast and heated,
full of shared lines and violent threats, and culminates with their
resolution to fight a duel. This simmering violence prepares the way
for the next scene.

214–34   This is Zanche's first aside in the play, signalling a significant shift in her relationship with the audience: she is now much
closer to us. Her sudden love for Francisco might be presented as
either comically endearing or as ridiculous; the choice made here
will have a significant impact upon our sympathy for her as the play
draws nearer to its conclusion.

This passage would, on the Jacobean stage, have been a distinctly
theatrical moment. The audience would have been presented with
two white male actors, both blacked-up, one playing a disguised
Duke and the other a woman. The characters were thus in many
senses parallel: both highly stylized, probably highly stereotyped,
and 'inauthentic'. Today, however, Francisco is likely to appear much
more self-consciously theatrical than Zanche, who will usually be
played by a black actress. Francisco's determination to use Zanche's

affection to 'draw strange fowl from this foul nest' (l. 134) may thus seem even more callous in modern performance now that Zanche is the more 'genuine' of the two.

Act V, scene ii

Act V is building in pace. If indeed the barriers for V.iii have already been set up (see notes to V.i.143–61), then this scene is a continuation of the previous one, and it leads directly into the action of V.iii, as Bracciano calls for his beaver for the fight. Playing the three consecutive scenes as a continuous sequence requires a slight foreshortening of time for Cornelia to have heard 'whispering all about the court' (l. 1), but this stretches the audience's credulity no more than previous scenes have done (IV.iii, for example, showed both the beginning and the end of the conclave). Marcello's murder may be a genuinely dramatic shock for an audience who have been primed to anticipate an entirely different murder (Bracciano's, by the conspirators).

1–13 Marcello – presumably still wound-up with anger – is attempting to evade Cornelia's questions regarding his forthcoming duel with Flamineo. The lines here suggest dynamic movement: 'Nay, I'll call the duke' (l. 7) implies that Cornelia is resorting to desperate measures to prevent Marcello from leaving the stage (presumably in search of Flamineo), while Marcello's reference to her crucifix (which probably hangs around her neck) suggests his proximity to her, following an abrupt return. The crucifix, of course, reminds us that these characters are associated with conventional Christian morality, while the story about the infant Flamineo breaking his mother's crucifix implies his innate evil – and, more specifically, his potential for violence towards her.

14–17 Flamineo's swift and brutal entrance, followed by an equally sudden exit, mirrors Cornelia's own in the previous scene (V.i.186–8) – though this appearance is more violent and its effect much more severe. Clearly Flamineo's anger is directed towards his brother, but this may be an act of revenge upon Cornelia just as much as it is on Marcello. Flamineo's killing of an unarmed man is dishonourable in the extreme. The actor will have to decide whether this is compounded by premeditation, or whether it has been provoked in some way by the heat of the moment. (Played straight, Flamineo's promise to 'send a surgeon' implies that he did not intend to murder his brother, but it might be played as a sarcastic taunt.) Cornelia's immediate responses are probably screams (ll. 14–15).

17–26 Marcello dies with conventional moral pronouncements, invoking divine retribution, and, in a final *sententia*, spurning social ambition. Superficially, we could be expected to agree with him: Hortensio's description of him as 'Virtuous Marcello' (l. 25) might seem to give voice to the play's own presentation of this character. However, Webster has complicated this otherwise straightforward view of Marcello over the last two scenes, when the character has behaved with spite and with unprovoked violence, and lied to his mother.

27–45 Webster shifts into yet another gear with this stark, almost naturalistic portrayal of a grieving mother in denial over her son's death. The heartbroken Cornelia speaks in devastatingly realistic prose, full of repetitions and simple, unaffected utterances. Gone is the dense, clever wordplay and complex verse we might usually associate with Webster's writing: what we are offered here is pure, unembellished grief. Interestingly, this sequence borrows heavily from the final scene of *King Lear*: Cornelia's refusal to believe that her child is dead echoes Lear's behaviour over his daughter Cordelia's corpse, and Cornelia's requests to seek signs of Marcello's breath using a looking-glass or a feather (ll. 38–40) quote directly from the earlier play (*King Lear*, V.iii.236–40). Her use of repetition is also reminiscent of Lear's language (see, for example, *King Lear*, V.iii.232 and 284).

46–61 Bracciano attempts to take control of the situation, trying to placate Cornelia by calling her 'mother' (it was common to use 'mother' to mean 'mother-in-law'). This only succeeds in tormenting Cornelia further, not only by reminding her of her daughter's marriage to a man of whom she clearly disapproves (see I.ii.285–90), but also by highlighting the loss of her son, who had called her 'mother' only seconds ago as he lay dying (l. 18). It is significant that Flamineo has not sought sanctuary in the Church as he indicated at line 16 – nor has he brought a surgeon. In a dramatic visual echo of

Marcello's murder, Cornelia attempts to run at her one remaining son with a knife – but unlike Flamineo, she '*lets it fall*'. The text leaves a lot up to the actor and the audience here. Are we meant to admire Cornelia's Christian forgiveness? And how is the silent Flamineo responding? Is he sorry?

61–70 Cornelia tries to suggest that Marcello's death was his own fault – presumably in order to prevent her other son from being executed for murder – but the Page speaks up to deny her account. It is not clear whether the Page was onstage to witness the murder – he may have been present from the beginning of the scene, but might simply have entered with Bracciano (which would keep the beginning of the scene a private exchange between mother and son). If the latter, his recognition of Cornelia's lie must be based on her behaviour rather than on his own knowledge of the facts.

71–84 Bracciano's edict that Flamineo will henceforth have to plead for his life each evening is a cruel means of ensuring that his servant does not turn against him – it might remind the audience of Flamineo's own description of his relationship with Zanche as holding 'a wolf by the ears...for fear of turning upon me' (V.i.155). Bracciano might even be played here as relishing the opportunity to exert some leverage over Flamineo, who has been in a position of considerable power until now, given his detailed knowledge of the Duke's actions. Lines 79–80 imply that Bracciano sees this action as revenge for Flamineo's insubordination at the house of convertites (IV.ii.44–71).

Bracciano is particularly unattractive here: there is no sense that justice is being served, but rather (as with Monticelso in Vittoria's trial) that powerful figures may use justice as a means of exerting and solidifying their own power. It is significant that the audience see Lodovico poison Bracciano's helmet at the very moment that this abuse of power takes place, and there is a kind of poetic justice in the method, which recalls Isabella's poisoning in II.ii. The exact process by which Lodovico applies the poison is unclear, but Webster's stage direction specifies that he 'sprinkles' it (l. 77 s.d.). Presumably, therefore, the poison is either in powdered form, or in a tiny vial of liquid; there may even be something rather mischievous and puckish about the image of Lodovico sprinkling it into the helmet.

Francisco's final aside shows his pleasure at the thought of Bracciano's damnation. If Bracciano puts on the poisoned helmet while he is still onstage, it will be a loaded moment for both Francisco and the audience.

Act V, scene iii

As the notes to V.ii have indicated, this scene could be played as a direct continuation of the action. It depicts the death of one of the central characters, but it is no tragic climax: the murder is already a *fait accompli* before the scene has begun, since Bracciano is already wearing the poisoned helmet, and any sense of nobility in defeat is undermined by Bracciano's protracted, gruesome death and a through-line of dark humour and cynicism.

1–5 The 'fight at barriers' happens suddenly, at the beginning of the scene, with no introduction. Five of the six participants are probably the Ambassadors, as Bracciano suggested at V.i.60–1; the remaining one is clearly Bracciano. A production might stage this as a lengthy and spectacularly choreographed fight sequence, with Bracciano slowly losing control of his body over the course of it; alternatively the sequence might be over relatively quickly, since there is no real dramatic need for tension here (Bracciano is already wearing the poisoned helmet). The first lines show Bracciano realizing the manner and method of his own poisoning, and he calls for his armourer to be tortured in a flurry of curt half-lines (imitating verbally the cut-and-thrust of the fight itself, perhaps).

6–28 Bracciano's dying observation that 'There are some great ones that have hand in this, / And near about me' (ll. 6–7) is truer than he realizes, and may be leant a sharper irony in performance by having 'Mulinassar' rush to his aid. The stage is full of activity, with Vittoria, Giovanni and the two Physicians crowding around Bracciano, while Flamineo orders the removal of the barriers behind them. Bracciano realizes his own impending death and faces it bravely, stage-managing the chaos around him by ordering Giovanni away and calling Vittoria to his side (ll. 16–17), but refusing to let her kiss him for fear of poisoning her (l. 26). His realization that 'This unction is sent from the great Duke of Florence' (l. 27) is accurate, and is once again underlain with irony as Francisco replies, 'Sir, be of comfort' (l. 28). Francisco's line has a double-meaning: superficially it is a line of reassurance, but it also means 'You can rest assured that your realization is true'.

29–41 Bracciano's words imply that Vittoria is weeping loudly: presumably he is clamouring to be heard over this noise. Lines 36–7 will often provoke a laugh in performance. Into this chaos enter the two ominous-looking Capuchins (really Lodovico and Gasparo). Flamineo's description of them as having 'brought the extreme unction' (l. 38) suggests that they forbode Bracciano's death, and they may approach him slowly as a visual metaphor of his impending demise. He is clearly horrified.

42–69 Left alone, Flamineo responds privately to his master's imminent death: once again, he uses the 'unofficial' register of prose. As we might expect, he takes a cynical view, pointing out that Bracciano's 'flatterers' will disappear as soon as he is no longer able to offer them advancement, and that their grief will not last long. Since we have only just seen Vittoria make a great display of weeping, we might suspect that Flamineo's condemnation implicates her, too. His comparison of himself to 'a wolf in a woman's breast' strengthens this: Vittoria herself was compared to a 'wolf' at IV.ii.92.

Flamineo's admission of disloyalty to Bracciano (ll. 57–9) and willingness to bad-mouth his dying employer (ll. 61–5) may be surprising to an audience, since Bracciano is not yet even dead. Francisco's responses to this behaviour will be interesting to watch: is he genuinely shocked by Flamineo's duplicity, or merely giving a show of being so, in keeping with his character, the honourable Mulinassar?

70–83 Lodovico enters with a description of the Duke's current state of mind, perhaps building the audience's anticipation of our final view of this character. When he reveals that Bracciano has 'conferred the whole state of the dukedom' upon Vittoria (ll. 79–80), Flamineo interprets this as good news – perhaps as an aside to the audience, but it would not be out of keeping with the previous sequence for him to admit this openly in front of Francisco and Lodovico. Played as an aside, however, it allows the actor playing Flamineo to re-establish his complicity with the audience (the stability of which may have been threatened by a counter-complicity between the audience and Francisco).

Bracciano's re-entrance, on a bed, is visually striking. The bed almost certainly emerges from the discovery space at the back of the stage, presenting a busy scene already in full-flow. It might recall the dumb-show of II.ii, in which Isabella entered '*in her nightgown as to bedward*' (23 s.d.) before being poisoned: it is a kind of poetic justice that Bracciano should die in similar circumstances. It may also remind the audience of the bed onto which Vittoria threw herself in IV.ii – a scene in which Bracciano made wild accusations similar to the ones he will make in the passage which follows. The stage direction indicates that Bracciano's speeches '*are several kinds of distractions and in the action should appear so*', indicating a physical portrayal of madness. This may have drawn from a vocabulary of conventional gestures which were recognizable and readable to the Jacobean audience (see also V.iv.82 s.d.).

84–130 Bracciano's dying ravings are, like many examples of stage madness in Jacobean drama, a mixture of sense and nonsense. Throughout the sequence, Vittoria and Flamineo's interjections are all half-lines, indicating a frantic pace.

At lines 84–6, Bracciano accuses somebody – probably either Vittoria or Flamineo – of a variety of crimes which might be committed by those in privileged social positions. His imaginings are highly symbolic, drawing on many of the play's key motifs: 'blackness' (l. 90), 'the devil' (ll. 90, 103), and dogs (ll. 93–7). He might, in his madness, half-recognize Francisco, prompting the reference to 'that politician Florence' at line 94; lines 98–106, meanwhile, allow a production great interpretive scope in choosing who (if anyone) Bracciano mistakes for the devil. His description of Vittoria's powdered hair is strikingly visceral, associating her with lust. The image of 'six grey rats that have lost their tails' (l. 124) creeping up the pillow towards him is an unsettling metaphor of impending death (and perhaps damnation – witches were believed to take the form of rats without tails).

His image of Flamineo is particularly apt: like a tightrope-walker carrying moneybags, Flamineo does indeed tread a dangerous and precarious path in order to secure his own advancement. Bracciano appears to condemn his follower for this behaviour, calling him a 'rogue' and suggesting that he should be hanged (ll. 110–16). In an aside which will probably provoke laughter, Flamineo confides his discomfort at being named by a dying man, interpreting it as 'a sign / I shall not live long' (ll. 129–30). He is correct: there are three disguised revengers on stage, ready and waiting.

131–51 Lodovico and Gasparo begin a long prayer in Latin (drawn from Erasmus's *Funus*), commending Bracciano's soul to heaven. Flamineo's and Vittoria's lines (132–5) draw the audience's attention to the crucifix, which must have a visual centrality and power here (Cornelia's crucifix was similarly foregrounded in V.ii.9–13). The Latin ritual seems holy and official, but of course the audience are fully aware that these are not really Capuchin monks: it is thus lent a sinister irony which verges on the blasphemous.

152–79 Left alone, the murderers reveal their true identities. They perform a reversal of the ritual they had previously been enacting – commending Bracciano's soul to heaven – by wishing him to the devil. The dialogue is punctuated by a quick interchange between speakers, as Lodovico and Gasparo continue one another's sentences (throughout, but especially at lines 157–64), giving the sense that Bracciano is being attacked from both sides not just literally but also verbally. The scene is pitiful: Bracciano is helpless, speechless and paralysed, while his murderers gloat and revel in his suffering and indignity. However despicable Bracciano's behaviour has been, it will be fairly impossible for an audience to find much to admire in his killers here.

It is up to the actor whether or not Bracciano recognizes his killers, or even understands them; if he does not, then the revenge is an empty one, but this may be dramatically effective and entirely in keeping with the play's themes. Either way, Bracciano is aware enough to call for Vittoria, prompting one of the scene's most darkly farcical moments: Gasparo hurries Vittoria and the attendants from the stage as soon as they enter, instructing Lodovico in a rushed aside to 'Strangle him in private' (l. 171). The audience will be on the edge of their seats, perhaps even exhilarated: the murder, when it finally comes, is as much a relief as anything else.

180–213   The second re-entrance of Vittoria and the attendants is as sudden and as brief as the first, and her abrupt exit is similar to I.ii.302. The stage is then emptied again for a second exchange between Francisco and Flamineo. The silent Lodovico is a threatening presence here: we have just seen him kill one man, and Webster has primed us to expect Flamineo's demise at any moment (see especially lines 128–30).

Flamineo gives voice to a misogynistic cynicism about the depth of Vittoria's grief; this might seem more than a little hypocritical of him, since his own disloyalty is manifest. Lines 188–90 make it clear that he considers his relationship with the Duke an investment which has failed to pay off. Is his bitterness here real, or a continuation of his feigned 'mad humour' (III.ii.306)? It seems incompatible with the desire he expresses at the end of this exchange to speak to Bracciano and 'shake him by the hand' (l. 212), and the implication that he will even pray for his dead employer. The actor playing Flamineo thus has a number of choices:

- Flamineo may be playing the role of 'malcontent' at the beginning of the exchange, before his real emotions surface. An eruption of genuine emotion would make Flamineo more sympathetic, and foreshadow the next scene (in which he will be both literally and metaphorically haunted).
- His apparent grief at the end may be insincere. This would be in keeping with the character's near-constant game-playing, and leave space for the character to develop later in the play.
- He may move from cynicism to genuine remorse over the course of the conversation. Such an interpretation would give a hint, in miniature, as to the character's later development.
- He may simply be feigning a number of contradictory attitudes throughout. This would be consistent with his self-described 'varying of shapes' (IV.ii.248).

Francisco deliberately turns the conversation back to himself: a dangerous strategy, but he seems confident that Flamineo is far from recognizing him. Flamineo's description of him as a 'Machivillain' (a conflation of 'Machiavellian' and 'villain') might be spoken with a trace of begrudging admiration (l. 194).

213–23　Francisco and Lodovico drop their disguises for a hurried conversation. Once again, they are quickly interrupted (and perhaps almost discovered) by the entrance of Zanche. This final change in tone allows the scene to finish on a comic note.

Lodovico's description of Zanche as 'the infernal' (l. 217) is a racist reference to her blackness, and one of many connections between dark skin and 'devils' (see V.i.86 and V.iii.89–91). The motif is, of course, a direct inversion of the 'white devil' of the play's title. Zanche herself employs this symbolism at the end of the scene, imagining that her betrayal of Vittoria will 'wash' her white (l. 263). In the Jacobean theatre, of course, the image had a literal reality: the white boy-actor playing Zanche might easily have washed off his black make-up. The lines are more problematic for a modern audience, who will be more sensitive to the lines' racist assumption of the innate superiority of white skin.

224–42　Zanche describes an erotically charged dream she claims to have had about 'Mulinassar'. The actor will have to decide whether Zanche really did have this dream, or whether she has invented it as the basis for a flirtatious conversation (the latter probably has more comic potential). Her description of the dream might remind the audience of Vittoria's employment of a similar strategy in I.ii.230–56, with Lodovico playing a similar role to that of Flamineo in the earlier scene – that of a sarcastic commentator speaking in asides both to his employer and to the audience.

The lines shared between Francisco and Zanche imply a shared energy which will almost certainly be sexual. Spatially, we probably see Zanche and Francisco in increasingly charged proximity to one another, while Lodovico lurks on the periphery of the stage, closer to the audience, making cynical asides. In this respect, Zanche, Francisco and Lodovico are directly echoing the dramaturgy of both I.ii.203–69 and IV.ii.72–223, mirroring the roles of Vittoria, Bracciano and Flamineo respectively.

243–71　The sequence climaxes with Zanche's confirmation of Vittoria and Flamineo's complicity in the murders of Isabella and Camillo (ll. 243–8), and her revelation that she intends to betray her mistress by stealing from her and escaping to the country (ll.

252–60). Her exit at line 264 allows Francisco and Lodovico to drop their acts, and once again, her almost immediate re-entrance catches them off-guard. The many near-misses and near-discoveries of this scene are likely to keep an audience in a state of tension, and create an edgy, even comic effect. Once she has exited for a second time, the scene ends with an anticipation of further vengeful 'action'.

Act V, scene iv

This is the second of the play's two ghost scenes, and like the previous one (IV.i), it serves to reposition its central character (in this case, Flamineo) in relation to the audience's sympathies. It may be that the appearance of Bracciano's ghost here is, like Francisco's encounter with Isabella's in IV.i, the product of a melancholy imagination. This scene is more ambiguous, however: Flamineo does not consciously summon the ghost in the way that Francisco did and, when he sees it, he reacts with surprise.

1–9   Webster begins this scene – clearly the beginning of the end for our protagonists – with another sequence which splits the stage between public performance (young Giovanni entering in his new role as Duke) and private conversation. Flamineo talks to Gasparo (who is presumably still in disguise as a Capuchin) about Giovanni, insulting the young Duke and suggesting that like his late father, he will grow to become dangerous before long. Once again, Webster uses a bird analogy to illustrate this: like an eagle, Giovanni's 'long tallants' (l. 8) will 'grow out in time' (l. 9).

10–31   Flamineo is addressing Giovanni directly from line 10, but it is not clear whether he has chosen this shift from unofficial speech to official, or whether the young Duke has interrupted Flamineo's unofficial conversation by his proximity. It may even be that Giovanni has overheard some of the conversation; this would certainly explain his coldness towards Flamineo here. He orders Flamineo to leave him, perhaps mindful of his disgraceful and dishonourable murder of Marcello.

Flamineo points out that since Giovanni has profited from Bracciano's death, he should 'be merry' (l. 12). Giovanni, who is perhaps already in black mourning attire, clearly takes offence at this cynical outlook, and orders Flamineo to 'Study your prayers, sir, and be penitent' (l. 21). This commentary has already discussed the problem of Giovanni's age (see notes to II.i.95–144). If a young child were to say these lines, Giovanni might seem implausibly precocious – though it might be in keeping with Giovanni's symbolic role as the embodiment of chivalry. On the other hand, an older Giovanni might more readily capture the young man's sudden increase in status, and in performance, we might gain a sense that Flamineo's expectation of Giovanni's future 'tallants' is in fact entirely accurate.

Left alone, Flamineo confides to the audience that he is 'falling to pieces' (l. 25). Our sympathy for him, however, may be somewhat strained by this point in the play. A production team will need to decide whether or not his observation that Giovanni has Francisco's 'villainous look' (l. 30) is accurate: it will strongly shape our responses to both Flamineo and Giovanni.

31–49 An unnamed courtier brings the news that Giovanni has just banished Flamineo from his presence. For Flamineo – who has spent almost the entire play wheedling himself into positions where he might be advanced by the powerful – this will be a shattering pronouncement. Superficially, he responds light-heartedly, with his usual riddling observations and bawdy jokes; in performance, however, we may see some evidence that the character is indeed 'falling to pieces' at this turn of events. It might rankle even more that the courtier, a heretofore unseen character, is now occupying the position which Flamineo would have wished for himself. After the courtier leaves, Flamineo's anger explodes, and he threatens violent reprisal.

50–65 Francisco enters and casts a different perspective on Flamineo's self-pity by reminding the audience (and Flamineo himself) of Marcello's murder and of Cornelia's grief. Once again, Webster builds up our expectation of an offstage event by having a character describe it in some detail before it is introduced to the stage. Whether or not we can trust in the sincerity of Francisco's description is open to question – he is speaking in his disguise as the more honourable Mulinassar. It is potent enough, however, to provoke Flamineo into wanting to observe the grief he has caused. His motivation for this is unclear: it will be up to the actor to decide whether the decision is driven by guilt, curiosity, spite, or something else.

66–113   Flamineo draws the curtain of the discovery space at the back of the stage, to reveal Cornelia, Zanche and three other ladies wrapping a shroud around Marcello's corpse (though in a modern performance, other means of 'discovering' this scene might be explored). The women either sing, or are accompanied by, a song which was not included in the printed text of the play. There is a strong case to be made for composing a replacement song in modern performance. This moment should act as a hiatus in the scene which is both visually arresting and emblematic.

The following sequence is almost a scene-within-a-scene, taking place as it does in a section of the stage space which was associated more with theatrical illusion than the more peripheral area which Flamineo now inhabits (as he does so often in the play). Flamineo and Francisco observe from a distance at first, perhaps moving closer as the scene progresses. Cornelia takes Flamineo's hand at line 82, though this may mean that she simply moves out from the discovery space. The stage direction – '*Cornelia doth this in several forms of distraction*' (l. 82) – implies a highly conventionalized style of acting (see notes to III.iii.1–7 and V.iii.70–83).

This scene's sense of theatricality is heightened by the fact that it quotes two very famous moments from other Renaissance plays featuring women in states of severe mental disturbance: IV.v from *Hamlet* and V.i from *Macbeth*. Like *Hamlet*'s Ophelia, Cornelia gives herbs and flowers (possibly imaginary ones) to those around her, drawing attention to their symbolic associations with sorrow and remembrance; some of her lines are almost direct quotations from Shakespeare's play (ll. 77, 113), and like Ophelia, she bursts into snatches of song. Noticing Flamineo, Cornelia moves into a pastiche of Lady Macbeth's sleepwalking scene, visualizing a 'white hand' which is metaphorically stained with blood (l. 82); unlike Lady Macbeth, though, Cornelia is examining another character's hand, rather than her own.

Cornelia's song at lines 96–105 contains some of the scene's most haunting language. The song initially invites friendly birds and woodland creatures to bury and protect an abandoned corpse (it is significant that she imagines Marcello's body as 'friendless', l. 99).

These lines are mournful, but it is not until the closing couplet that the imagery really bites. Cornelia imagines a 'wolf' ready to dig up her son's corpse 'with his nails' (104–5). The metaphor suggests a lurking evil, and might be played as an insinuation of Flamineo's guilt.

The reactions of the other characters will be fascinating here. Flamineo is relatively silent (which is notable in itself), noticeably separate from the scene he watches. Webster specifies that Cornelia gives rue – a symbol of sorrow and repentance – to the heretofore unrepentant Flamineo. He does not answer straight away, indicating perhaps that his mother's words and actions are indeed provoking feelings of remorse in him. When she mistakes him for a 'grave-maker', his one-word response – 'So' – shows none of his usual cynical wit (l. 80). His wish that he 'were from hence' (l. 92) indicates that he has indeed been unsettled by this turn of events. Cornelia's words are pointed and ironic enough that it is possible for an actor to suggest that on some level, she knows what she is doing to her son.

Another key figure here is Zanche, who we should remember is *Vittoria's* servant, not Cornelia's. Quite why she is involved in this act of ritual mourning is unclear: perhaps she has been appointed by Vittoria to care for the demented Cornelia. The last time we saw these characters together, of course, was during Cornelia's vicious physical attack on Zanche at V.i.186. We may sense an element of *schadenfreude* (pleasure in others' pain) from Zanche here: her observation that 'Her ladyship's foolish' (l. 74) might be spoken with relish, and her two attempts to get Cornelia to recognize Flamineo may be the kind of 'uncharity' which Francisco warned against at line 62.

The sequence might end with Cornelia retreating back into the discovery space and 'shutting up shop' (l. 112) by drawing the curtain back across in front of her. If so, it is significant that she retreats into the space from which the earlier dumb-shows emerged – she disappears into a space associated with both death and the absence of language. As she shuts off her busy and highly theatrical scene-within-a-scene, the stage is left bare and empty again – and probably seems even emptier than before. This paves the way for Flamineo's moment of epiphany.

114–24 Left alone to ponder the human consequences of his actions, Flamineo acknowledges – perhaps to Francisco, perhaps to the audience – that he is experiencing compassion for the first time in his life. He asks Francisco to leave him, and then he continues his exploration of this new-found remorse, admitting to the audience that he has lived 'Riotously ill' – adding, in what must have been a politically loaded statement for the Jacobean audience, 'like some that live in court' (l. 120). Unlike the prose with which he opened the scene, Flamineo now speaks in verse: indicating, perhaps, that he is now expressing a more noble side to his nature.

His couplet at lines 123–4 concludes with an observation about 'caged birds' which resonates with many of the play's characters who are trapped in some way in the machinery of power. Audiences might be reminded of Flamineo's earlier use of a bird-cage metaphor, in which he implied that characters (like himself) who were outside the 'bird-cage' would 'despair to get in', while characters who were already 'inside' would be 'in a consumption for fear they shall never get out' (I.ii.43–6). His language here implies that now that he has come so close to being 'inside', he is having second thoughts as to whether it is really what he wants at all (confirming his earlier observation). The couplet is aphoristic and arresting, and might sound to an audience like the end of the scene.

125–42   Webster surprises the audience with a second visual 'reveal'. Bracciano's ghost enters in the traditional costume of a Renaissance stage ghost, loaded with visual emblems: the Jacobean audience would have recognized the 'pot of lily-flowers with a skull in't' as a common symbol of a sinful, lust-filled life, doomed to end in death and damnation. His act of throwing earth upon Flamineo and of showing him the skull carries a meaning which is still obvious today. Images of death have permeated the language of the play so far: now, these images are made manifest. The tone of the scene shifts from the sombre to the sensational.

Flamineo's reaction is interesting: after momentary surprise (as indicated by his 'Ha!'), he appears to accept the presence of the ghost and respond with a defiance which recalls his behaviour at IV.ii.51 (when Bracciano asked, 'Do you stand me?'). The words 'Nearer, nearer yet' (l. 125) may simply mean that Bracciano's ghost is advancing on Flamineo, or it could be that Flamineo is mustering up the courage to approach him himself. The ghost remains silent in the face of Flamineo's questions: should we interpret him as the real spirit of Bracciano, or a product of Flamineo's imagination? The play has already presented a ghost sequence as an act of melancholic imagination – when Isabella appeared to Francisco at IV.i.102–15 – and the parallels between the characters are striking, with both Flamineo and Francisco having played comparably manipulative yet peripheral roles in the play's action, and having exhibited similarly cynical attitudes. Like Francisco, Flamineo considers 'melancholy' as a possible cause of the ghost's appearance (l. 144; see also IV.i.101), but whereas Francisco remained in control of his apparition, Flamineo seems convinced that this one is from a source 'beyond' his own imagination (l. 144).

A modern production will need to decide whether or not to present Bracciano's ghost in the same manner as Isabella's in terms of movement, lighting and stage space; either way, it will have implications as to the 'reality' of this occurrence. A parallel might also be drawn between Bracciano's ghost and Cornelia's madness. As twin catalysts of Flamineo's emotional epiphany, it might be suitable for both revelations to be 'discovered' in the same area of the stage.

143–52   The ghost departs, leaving Flamineo energized and perhaps a little *less* repentant than he was at lines 114–24. Daring fate to 'do its worst' (l. 146), Flamineo draws his weapon (though he may have drawn it already at the sight of the ghost) and leaves the stage resolved to confront Vittoria. His threat to kill her if she does not do him 'good' (l. 152) is almost a promise to the audience, who must be aware that they are now approaching the end of this tragedy.

Act V, scene v

This short scene builds on the audience's expectations of the impending denouement. It maintains the pace by rushing through two major plot points – Francisco's last appearance in the play, and the discovery of the revenge plan – in only 15 lines. The scene depicts yet another furtive conversation, and like I.ii.206–70 (and possibly IV.iii.80–130), it features an unseen eavesdropper.

1–11   Lodovico and Francisco speak to one another in secret, in their own identities. If they are still wearing their disguises, they might remove these; Lodovico will resume his in the final scene, but Francisco has no more need of his. The sight of Francisco having removed (or perhaps just partially removed) his black make-up might recall Zanche's line at V.iii.263.

Their alliance appears to remain a fraught one: Lodovico resorts to threats in order to persuade Francisco to leave, and the characters' separate exits give a very literal sense that Lodovico and Francisco are now going their separate ways. Francisco's parting words remind the audience that Lodovico's life is not safe either: indeed, revenge tragedies conventionally conclude with the death of the revenger as well as of the wrongdoers.

12–15   Hortensio recognises that 'some black deed' is being planned (l. 12). The conversation he has overheard did not make it clear whose 'murder' (l. 8) was being discussed, though the audience – and perhaps Hortensio – might reasonably guess that it was Vittoria's. Hortensio's closing words are yet another reminder of the mortal danger faced by most of the remaining major characters in the final scene.

Act V, scene vi

The final scene plays with the audience's anticipation of Vittoria's death, repeatedly subverting our expectations. First, we are led to believe that Flamineo will kill Vittoria; she then appears to get the better of him, apparently shooting him dead. Then he rises, as if from the dead, to reveal that it was a trick, and we begin to suspect that he will now kill her for real. Webster surprises us yet again by bringing in the assassins at this pivotal moment. The scene keeps the audience in a state of tension throughout, and uses comedy to release this tension at strategic points.

1–21   Vittoria is reading some kind of devotional book (perhaps a Bible), attended by Zanche, when Flamineo bursts in on them. He is probably in exactly the same physical state in which we saw him last: invigorated, ready for violence, with his weapon drawn. Line 3 indicates a flurry of physical activity: Vittoria might attempt to rise as Flamineo forces her to sit, while Zanche presumably attempts to leave before Flamineo orders her to stay. (His use of the insulting term 'blowze' indicates that his affection for her has worn thin.) Virtually every change in speaker occurs mid-line, indicating a frenetic pace.

We have not seen much of Vittoria since Marcello's death, and the little we have seen was her response to Bracciano's poisoning. Her greeting of Flamineo as 'ruffin' (l. 1), her reference to the biblical story of Cain and Abel (ll. 13–14) and her accusation that he is 'a villain' (l. 15) indicate that she is genuinely appalled by his actions. Readers might notice that the play has given us almost no indication as to the kind of relationship Vittoria had with Marcello. He expressed disapproval of her actions at III.i.32–6 and (by implication) at V.ii.20–2, and was present at both her trial and her marriage, but Webster gives them no conversations at all. A director will have to decide whether this absent relationship is worth exploring through body language and unscripted interaction in performance; if it is, it will have its pay-off in this exchange.

Flamineo is clearly angered (though perhaps not surprised) by his sister's refusal to reward him. His description of Vittoria as having 'a devil' in her (l. 18) once again links her – at a pivotal moment – with the play's title. He leaves the stage with a riddling threat.

22–55   Flamineo's re-entrance with 'two case' (two pairs) of pistols is a classic theatrical device. Upon seeing a pistol onstage, audiences will often enter a state of physical tension in anticipation of the inevitable gunshot; here, Webster keeps his audience in this state for quite some time. To the Jacobean audience, in fact, the convention would have aroused even more tension: whereas modern audiences can generally be confident that no-one in the theatre will really be harmed by an onstage firearm, the audiences of the Renaissance had no such reassurance. A letter written by a playgoer named Philip Gawdy in 1587 reports the deaths of two audience members and the wounding of a third after a gun misfired in a performance by the Lord Admiral's Men (see Gurr 2004: 67).

Flamineo may point a pistol at Vittoria, or he might have one trained on each of the two women; alternatively, the pistols may be in their cases, as is suggested by the comparison with jewels (l. 24). However he brings them in, he certainly has one trained on Vittoria by line 28, as her response indicates. His speeches at lines 31–41 are lies: we never saw Bracciano demand Vittoria's murder, and even if he had, we are familiar enough with Flamineo's character by this point that we know that he would never promise his own suicide in earnest. Vittoria assumes her brother is sincere, attributing his behaviour to 'melancholy and despair' (l. 42) – she speaks carefully and concisely, aware that one misjudged word might result in her death.

Zanche has established by line 55 that they are locked in: she may have realized this at the beginning of the scene, or alternatively (if Flamineo is entirely focused on Vittoria here) she may have attempted escape following his re-entrance with the pistols. She informs Vittoria of their entrapment in an aside.

56–75 Vittoria and Zanche try to save themselves from Flamineo by employing a number of different strategies. Vittoria attempts to reason with him, scaring him with thoughts of mortality and damnation (ll. 56–64, 65–7); in the middle of her speech, however, she quietly commands Zanche to call for help (l. 61). When Zanche does so, Flamineo finds a way of stopping her, presumably either with physical violence or with a threat to that effect (ll. 64–5).

In a third exchange of asides, Zanche advises Vittoria to 'seem to consent' to Flamineo's wishes, and Vittoria agrees to this plan (ll. 72–5). The ease with which these two women switch between public speaking and private plotting in this scene – in one case, within one sentence (ll. 58–64) – is a testament to their cleverness, but might also have been seen by members of the Jacobean audience as justifying Flamineo's misogynistic views about women's duplicity.

76–118 During this sequence, all three characters onstage are being insincere. All of them make ostensibly noble dying speeches, professing their love for, and solidarity with, one another. The audience have been made aware of Vittoria and Zanche's plan, but will not be certain what Flamineo is up to; in any case, we know that all is not as it seems on the surface. Both women swear 'Most religiously' not to outlive Flamineo (l. 99), and though they have no intention of keeping their oath, both will prove true to their words by the end of the scene. Flamineo builds up to the shooting with an overblown speech, moving from rhetorical prose to verse. The women take two pistols each, each pointing one at the other, and one at Flamineo – the three characters must therefore move into a triangular stage arrangement. They fire the pistols on his command, leading to the first climax of the scene.

119–47 Vittoria and Zanche have clearly understood one another's intentions to shoot Flamineo, but to spare themselves. They betray

their treachery immediately, running to the fallen Flamineo in order
to '*tread upon him*' (l. 118 s.d.). As they taunt him in what they presume
are his dying moments, the audience will probably be reminded
of Lodovico and Gasparo's treatment of the dying Bracciano at
V.iii.151–68. Like the conspirators, Vittoria and Zanche take great
pleasure in telling their victim that he is damned, reminding him of
his 'villainies' and completing one another's sentences as they do so.
In performance, the scene may well employ similar staging.

Flamineo's lines become increasingly histrionic over this, and
if an audience do not suspect him of deceit at the beginning of the
sequence, they may well do by the time he reaches his darkly funny
'death' speech, in which he describes his liver as 'parboiled like
Scotch holy bread' and the pain as like 'a plumber laying pipes in
my guts' (ll. 143–4). An actor will have to decide whether Flamineo's
insincerity is obvious or not: if it is too obvious, it risks undermining
the gloriously theatrical surprise which follows.

148–67   Flamineo's behaviour suddenly changes, as he drops his
ludicrous death speech and reveals that there were no bullets in the
pistols. The moment will almost certainly make an audience laugh,
but a director will have to decide whether the revelation should be a
sudden or a prolonged one (Flamineo might turn his 'dying' gasps
into laughter before speaking, for example, or he might simply get
up and brush himself off). This opportunity for a release of the audience's tension through laughter is an effective dramatic technique,
paving the way for a more intense tragic climax which will not be
counteracted by laughter a second time.

Flamineo's behaviour should make more sense to an audience
now: this was a test of Vittoria and Zanche's loyalty to him (a test
which they have clearly failed quite spectacularly). This gives him
another excuse to launch into a misogynistic diatribe, before he
produces two more pistols with which he presumably intends to
murder the women for real. With the production of the third pair of
pistols – these ones, we must assume, fully loaded – Webster achieves
the same tense effect a second time.

168–83   This time, however, our expectation of gunshots is undermined. Four of the conspirators enter, having had keys made especially. They might enter from one door or from two, and they
presumably surround Flamineo and the women with their swords

82

drawn. The fact that Flamineo does not fire his pistols implies that they disarm him before he can respond.

The audience are now provided with one of the scene's key dramatic pay-offs: the moment at which Lodovico and Gasparo throw off their disguises and reveal that they have been employed by Francisco. The reactions of Flamineo, Vittoria and Zanche are hugely important here: Flamineo because he has been outwitted, Vittoria because this spells her inevitable death and Zanche because the man she thought she loved (and for whom she betrayed her mistress) is revealed to have been Francisco in disguise.

183–232 Each of the conspirators except Pedro (who does not speak) seems to have been assigned a different character to dispatch: the dialogue suggests that Gasparo deals with Vittoria, Lodovico with Flamineo and Carlo with Zanche. We might thus see three linked but separate dramas unfolding in miniature at once. Vittoria tries to plead with Gasparo, but to no avail (ll. 183–9); Lodovico, meanwhile, attempts to gloat over Flamineo, but is undermined when Flamineo responds by laughing – a direct inversion of the moment earlier in the play when Lodovico broke his melancholic 'covenant' with Flamineo by laughing at him (III.iii.101–22). He then turns to taunt Vittoria, and his words – 'glorious strumpet' (l. 206) and 'prodigious comet' (l. 214) – suggest a strange combination of contempt and admiration.

Vittoria's insistence that she should enter the afterlife ahead of her servant might recall Cleopatra's behaviour in the final scene of Shakespeare's *Antony and Cleopatra*. In death, her greatest qualities return to the surface: she is brave, proud and defiant. Zanche follows suit: called a 'black Fury' by her captor (perhaps because she is fighting back), she dies with a pronouncement of equality ('I have blood / As red as either of theirs', ll. 227–8) and a statement of her pride in her blackness (229–31). Lodovico orders the conspirators to strike at their victims all at once, 'With a joint motion' (l. 232).

232–76 The exact manner of the three victims' deaths is not made clear in the text. They are 'struck', presumably by the conspirators' swords, and while Vittoria and Flamineo take some time to die of their wounds, Zanche is presumably dead by the time Flamineo speaks lines 253–4. Whether she dies immediately, or slowly and quietly, will be up to the director.

Both Vittoria and Flamineo defy their killers even as they die: Vittoria mocks them as cowardly (describing their actions in ironic terms as 'manly' before equating them with child-killers), and Flamineo jokes that they have not stabbed him deeply enough, even going so far as to inquire after the maker of the blade. Both responses potentially undermine the conspirators' sense of revenge.

Vittoria's dying recognition that her 'greatest sin' lay in her 'blood' (l. 240) may be a conventional repentance of her lust, but the line is ambiguous: 'blood' might be taken to mean either 'temper' or 'family', too, and both meanings are equally applicable. An actor might choose to make the meaning clear in performance, or to leave it ambiguous. Vittoria's final words take the form of a *sententia* in a rhyming couplet, blaming her misfortune on her closeness to the court (ll. 261–2). Flamineo, meanwhile, dies with a new-found (or at least rediscovered) admiration for his sister – though in keeping with his misogyny, he sees her positive qualities in terms of their masculinity (ll. 242–7). When he picks up her metaphor of a doomed ship in order to comfort her as she dies, it implies that he has found a heartfelt sympathy for her.

Flamineo's 'real' death speech is a marked contrast from his 'fake' one at lines 141–5. He speaks in highly charged and metaphorical verse, and expresses an individualistic sentiment which would have sounded frighteningly modern to a Jacobean audience: 'at myself I will begin and end' (l. 258). When Vittoria dies, his flowing verse gives way to a burst of cynical prose about the dangers of 'great men' (l. 265), and suddenly he occupies the here-and-now of Jacobean London by making reference to the Tower of London (l. 266) – the moment breaks both the rhythm and the illusion of the scene quite abruptly. Returning to verse for a climactic and theatrical finish, he repents the 'black charnel' that was his life (l. 270), and makes a final joke about having lost his voice (which may be played as a meta-theatrical joke by an actor who has, after all, spoken a large proportion of the play's lines). Finally, in a moment which once again draws meta-theatrical attention to the construction of the play itself, he addresses his killers as 'glorious villains' (l. 272) and seems to call for a dramatic sound effect, inviting the 'thunder' to 'strike loud' as his death-knell (l. 276). This rounds off the play's many references to thunder, which began in the first scene (I.i.11–12).

277–301   Flamineo's invocation of thunder anticipates the round of shooting which will conclude the play. Giovanni's guards are led in by the English Ambassador, who orders them to fire at the conspirators; Lodovico is wounded, as presumably are the others. This is a literal case of 'shooting first and asking questions later': Giovanni interrogates the conspirators in a very quick round of questions and answers before sending them away 'to prison, and to torture' (l. 291). Lodovico relishes his achievement despite his impending torture (ll. 293–7).

The play concludes conventionally, with the re-establishment of social order by the play's surviving representatives of traditional morality: the young Giovanni, who was presented as a chivalric ideal upon his first appearance in II.i, and the English Ambassador, who, we should remember, functioned as a kind of spokesperson for the audience during Vittoria's trial in III.ii. But there is more than a grain of uneasiness in this ending. Giovanni's use of force and violent retribution here is different from the merciful approach he discussed with his uncle and his father at II.i.127–36, and Flamineo's anticipation that the young prince would grow 'tallants' (talons) in time (V.iv.8–9) seems to have come true sooner than even Flamineo expected.

The audience may be left with a profound sense of irresolution. What will happen to Francisco? Will Giovanni attempt to punish his uncle, as his words at lines 290–3 imply? Is this merely the beginning of further bloodshed between factions? Or will Francisco manage to resume the close relationship with his nephew which we saw earlier in the play? And what has happened to Monticelso? The play's ending seems to imply that punishment is for the disenfranchised: the powerful can remain corrupt, and get away with it. In this respect, it is a powerful and politically provocative challenge to the conventions of tragic drama.

3   *Intellectual and Cultural Context*

Webster's career

Little is known for certain of Webster's life, though certain educated guesses can be made. He was born around 1579, to John and Elizabeth Webster of the London parish of St Sepulchre's. His father was a prosperous coach-maker and a member of a prestigious guild, the Company of Merchant Taylors. This comfortable middle-class background meant that young Webster would have encountered a wide cross-section of Elizabethan society as he grew up: his father must have provided carts for the prisons as well as coaches for the aristocracy, and served customers of every social stratum in between. Later in his career, Webster's class background would be referred to in a satirical poem by Henry Fitzjeffrey, in which he was (somewhat sneeringly) described as 'Crabbed Websterio / The Playwright Cartwright' (*Satyres and Satyricall Epigrams*, 1617).

His father's guild membership makes it very likely that Webster attended the Merchant Taylors' School, where he would have been educated in the vernacular English language before learning Latin, and would almost certainly have participated in dramatic performances. The boys of the school had a good reputation as an acting troupe, and former pupils included the playwrights Thomas Kyd and Thomas Lodge. Webster's education probably continued at the Middle Temple, which admitted a student by the name of John Webster in 1598: there, he would have trained in the legal profession. Law would certainly become a recurring theme in his plays.

London's new theatre industry had flourished during Webster's formative years. The first purpose-built London playhouse, The Theatre, had been built in 1576, with its rival The Curtain opening the following year; Webster, therefore, was born into a city in which the theatre business had already taken root. By the turn of the century, the Rose, the Globe and the Swan, all open-air public playhouses, had been built on Bankside, and the Fortune had opened north of the river. A number of indoor theatres were also in use by companies of child actors.

It is not known precisely when or how the young Webster side-stepped into this burgeoning industry, but by 1602 he was firmly entrenched as a regular collaborative dramatist. The diary of the theatre entrepreneur Philip Henslowe lists Webster as co-author of no less than three different plays for the Rose Theatre: *Caesar's Fall* (with Thomas Dekker, Michael Drayton, Thomas Middleton and Anthony Munday), *Lady Jane* (with Thomas Heywood) and *Christmas Comes But Once a Year* (with Heywood, Dekker and Henry Chettle). All three of these plays are now lost, though *Lady Jane* has probably survived in adapted form as *The Famous History of Sir Thomas Wyatt*. This play, based on the life of Lady Jane Grey (the 'Nine Days' Queen'), depicts its central female character as a political pawn who is ultimately destroyed by the powerful men around her. It might therefore be seen as an early prototype of Webster's two most famous tragedies, *The White Devil* and *The Duchess of Malfi*.

Lady Jane aside, Webster's earliest surviving works are different from the plays for which he is most famous. *Westward Ho!* was a popular city comedy, written for indoor performance by the St Paul's Boys in 1604 in collaboration with Thomas Dekker. Its success led Webster to co-write with Dekker once again, producing the follow-up *Northward Ho!* for the same company the following year. Both plays are satirical portraits of contemporary middle-class London life, drawing perhaps on Webster's own background. The influence of city comedy on Webster's tragedies, while faint, can nonetheless be traced in scenes such as Flamineo's orchestration of his master's extra-marital affair in *The White Devil* (I.ii).

It is not clear precisely what Webster did in the years between the completion of *Northward Ho!* and the eventual performance and publication of his next play, *The White Devil*, in 1612. Webster acknowledges in the latter's preface, 'To the Reader', that he 'was a long time in finishing this tragedy', and suggests that his writing is aimed at long-lasting acclaim rather than short-lived prolificacy. Indeed, the writing style of *The White Devil* suggests a painstaking process of compilation, composed as it is of an extraordinary synthesis of quotations and 'borrowings' from literally hundreds of different sources (see 'Webster's sources', below). However, it is also likely that Webster was simply unable to secure many commissions during these years: public theatrical performances were, as M. C. Bradbrook notes, banned for 33 of the 60 months between January 1606 and December 1610 due to outbreaks of plague (1980: 123).

The White Devil was evidently not well-received upon its first performances (see Chapter 1), and the fact that Webster put it into print almost straight away indicates that he must have felt the play had a greater chance of success as a work of literature than as a piece of theatre. He published *A Monumental Column*, an elegy for the death of Prince Henry, in late 1612, in which he borrowed heavily from his then-unfinished tragedy *The Duchess of Malfi*. *The Duchess of Malfi* was performed by the King's Men at both the indoor Blackfriars Theatre and the outdoor Globe, probably around 1614. It seems to have been rather more successful with its audience than *The White Devil* had been only a year or two earlier at the Red Bull.

Webster seems not to have returned to single-authored tragedy after this (or if he did, the work has been lost). He wrote a tragi-comedy, *The Devil's Law-Case*, in 1619, and then returned to collaborative writing after that. He co-wrote a further city comedy, *Anything for a Quiet Life*, with Thomas Middleton in 1620, and collaborated on a number of tragedies and tragicomedies in the early 1620s. In 1624, he wrote and co-ordinated a pageant for the new Lord Mayor of London – a member of the Merchant Taylors' Company. There is no record of Webster's death, but he is referred to in the past tense in Heywood's *Hierarchie of the Blessed Angels* in 1634, which implies that he was dead by then.

Jacobean tragedy

The White Devil is advertised on its title page as a 'Tragedy', placing it within a broad but distinctive literary and theatrical genre. Tragedy was enormously popular on the Jacobean stage, so it is worth considering exactly what the word might have meant to Webster's audience.

One of the earliest and most influential definitions of tragedy is that given by the classical philosopher Aristotle in his *Poetics* (c. 335 BC). Aristotle described tragedy as 'an imitation of an action that is serious, complete, and of a certain magnitude', and identified several key components of a tragic plot: these included the *hamartia*, the *anagnorisis* and the *peripeteia*. The *hamartia* is an error or sin made by the protagonist early on in the drama, sometimes knowingly but often unknowingly; this fault then instigates a series of actions which lead, eventually, to a *peripeteia*, or reversal, in which the protagonist's fortunes change dramatically (and often suddenly) from good to bad. This moment is often accompanied by an *anagnorisis*: a moment of recognition or realization. The chorus in Aeschylus' play *Agamemnon* sums up the conclusion of classical tragedy thus: 'Men shall learn wisdom, by affliction schooled' (216–18). The audience, moved to pity and fear by the drama, will ideally be led to what Aristotle calls *catharsis*: a kind of cleansing of these emotions.

Certainly one can see this pattern, or something like it, at work in much Jacobean tragedy. Well-known tragedies like *King Lear*, *Macbeth* and *Othello* feature heroes who make great errors of judgement in the first act of the play, only to realize their mistakes too late. One might see Webster's Vittoria and Flamineo as protagonists in the same mould: both consciously choose a 'sinful' path in Act I, apparently reaching comfort and security by the beginning of Act V, but realizing by the end of the play's final scene that their actions have brought about their ruin.

There is a strong ethical dimension to this pattern, of course. The tragic protagonist, in living out the fatal consequences of a grave moral error, might be seen to be giving instruction to the audience by example. Webster's several-time co-writer Thomas Heywood suggested as much in *An Apology for Actors*, published in 1612 (the same year as *The White Devil*); he described tragedy as 'the fatal and abortive ends of such as commit notorious murders, which is aggravated and acted with all the art that may be, to terrify men from the like abhorred practices'. The moral of tragedy, he concluded, was 'to persuade men to humanity and good life...showing them the fruits of honesty and the end of villainy'. As the protagonist of *The Revenger's Tragedy* (1607) puts it: 'When the bad bleeds, then is the tragedy good' (III.v.206).

But 'good' and 'bad' are elastic categories, and nowhere is this more evident than in Jacobean tragedy itself. The laws of God and the laws of the state were officially one and the same in Jacobean England; as James I himself put it in a speech to Parliament in 1610, 'to dispute what God may do is blasphemy,...so is it sedition in subjects to dispute what a king may do in the height of his power'. Superficially, many Jacobean tragedies might be seen to illustrate the dangerous consequences of abandoning the laws of God and state: Macbeth, for example, murders the King, God's representative; Lear, in abdicating, also flouts the established order; Flamineo and Vittoria wilfully reject traditional morality in order to advance themselves; and all of these characters pay a terrible price. John Ford's *'Tis Pity She's a Whore* (1633) expresses the principle of divine retribution, suggesting that though 'Great men may do their wills...Heaven will judge them for't another day' (III.ix.70–71). Sin against the prevailing social order, these tragedies seem to say, and you will suffer the consequences both in this life and in the next.

On the other hand, many tragedies of the period contain potentially subversive challenges to the social status quo. Both *Doctor Faustus* and *'Tis Pity She's a Whore* depict potentially sympathetic atheist characters, while the plot of Webster's own *The Duchess of Malfi* seems to illustrate the argument that true nobility is in a person's actions, not their birth. As the character Bosola puts it:

> Some would think the souls of princes were brought forth by some more weighty cause than those of meaner persons. They are deceived. There's the same hand to them; the like passions sway them. (II.i.101–5)

The White Devil espouses some similarly radical ideas:

> ... what difference is between the Duke and I? No more than between two bricks: all made of one clay. Only't may be one is placed on the top of a turret, the other in the bottom of a well by mere chance. (V.i.106–9)

Tragedy, then, might offer the possibility for the subversion of what appear to be the genre's core assumptions.

A complicating factor in this analysis of tragedy is the existence of a particular sub-genre – to which *The White Devil* almost certainly belongs – known as 'revenge tragedy'. Inspired by the tragedies of the

Roman playwright Seneca, Elizabethan dramatists developed a tragic form which focused on the private revenge of a protagonist who had been the victim of a terrible injustice. Perhaps the most influential of these was Thomas Kyd's *The Spanish Tragedy*: written in the late 1580s, this revenge play was reprinted at least ten times over the next four decades, and became the single most quoted play of the period. Its heady mix of political intrigue, ghostly visitations, plotting, madness and bloody recrimination would resurface in several tragedies of the period, including *The Revenger's Tragedy* and Shakespeare's *Titus Andronicus* and *Hamlet*. J. W. Lever has described the format thus: 'a wide range of characters, a court setting, a dynamic of complicated intrigue and delayed revenge, with a final spectacular catastrophe' (1971: 81). *The White Devil*, of course, is atypical in that its 'revenger' characters (Lodovico and Francisco) are not usually seen as its protagonists.

Revenge tragedy is unlike classical tragedy in that the revenger often experiences no *anagnorisis*, or realization: he tends to be as determined to fulfil his vengeful mission at the end of the play as he was at the beginning, dying as he completes it. It may be, however, that the protagonist's very willingness to take up the call to revenge is his *hamartia*; revenge tragedy thus presents its audience with a thorny moral ambiguity as the protagonist is torn between the contradictory imperatives of private honour and public law. As philosopher Francis Bacon put it in his essay 'Of Revenge' in 1597, 'Revenge is a kind of wild justice, which the more man's nature runs to, the more ought the law to weed it out' (1972: 13). The revenger is caught between irreconcilable values: on the one hand, he is honour-bound to avenge; on the other, Christian morality dictates that he should not commit murder. This difficulty is explored in *Hamlet* especially.

Renaissance tragedy is famously graphic in its presentation of death and violence. Gruesome physical images are widespread: the rape, cannibalism, severed body parts and general slaughter of plays such as *The Spanish Tragedy*, *The Changeling*, *Edward II*, *Titus Andronicus*, *King Lear* and *Macbeth* are examples enough. Images of cruelty in *The Duchess of Malfi* alone include a severed hand, strangled babies, howling madmen, and a report of the Duke having turned mad and dug up the leg of a dead man, howling 'fearfully' (V.ii.12–15). Murders are frequently presented with horrific ingenuity: *The Revenger's Tragedy* features a poisoned skull, *The Duchess of Malfi* a poisoned Bible and *Arden of Faversham* (like *The White Devil*) a poisoned painting.

The effect of all this brutality on stage is often to paint a bleak portrait of human society. King Lear famously asks of the 'poor bare, forked animal' he sees before him, 'Is man no more than this?' (III.iv.103, 108). *'Tis Pity She's a Whore* does much to emphasize a similar view – man is described as 'A wretch, a worm, a nothing' (I.i.76). Iago refers to humans in terms of animal imagery throughout *Othello*, finally driving Othello himself to talk about people in similar terms, and *The White Devil* too is loaded with images of human beings as animals or birds. It may be that the effect of such images is to purge the audience of their socially destructive 'black and deep desires' (*Macbeth*, I.iv.58); on the other hand, it may be that they open up some deeper, more radical questions about power and violence.

A central figure in Jacobean tragedy is the 'malcontent'. This character appears frequently in plays of the period, usually as a man born into high social status who has somehow lost his position, and has become an educated but impoverished outsider. His outsider status leads him at once both to desire social advancement and to disdain the system which continues to exclude him, and he usually displays a cynical and satirical attitude towards social norms. A notable example is Malevole, the title character of John Marston's *The Malcontent* (c. 1603); Webster himself wrote a new 'Induction' to this play when it was acquired by the King's Men in 1604, and was almost certainly influenced by its combination of revenge tragedy and satire, in which political intrigue and sexual corruption mix with cynicism and dark humour. The satirical voice of Flamineo owes much to this stage tradition, and would resurface in the character of Bosola in *The Duchess of Malfi*.

Webster's sources

As a dramatist, Webster was something of a magpie. He evidently read widely and kept extensive notes, since his plays are filled with quotations from a wide variety of different sources. The extent of his intertextuality is illustrated in the following excerpt from R. W. Dent's painstaking study *John Webster's Borrowings* (1960), in which

Dent maps a brief passage from *The White Devil* (III.ii.141–51) against some of its literary sources:

Monticelso. Well, well, such counterfeit jewels
Make true ones oft suspected.
Vittoria. You are deceived.

More: "many well counterfeited jewels make ye true mistrusted." [Sir Thomas More, *The History of King Richard III*, c. 1513]

For know that all your strict-combined heads,
Which strike against this mine of diamonds,
Shall prove but glassen hammers; they shall break, –
These are but feigned shadows of my evils.

Matthieu, of conspirators against Henry IV: "those heads which shall strike against this rock of Diamant will prove Glass." [Pierre Matthieu et al., 'Continuation' of Jean de Serres, *A General Inventorie of the Historie of France unto 1598*, tr. E. Grimeston, 1607]

Terrify babes, my lord, with painted devils;
I am past such needless palsy. For your names
Of whore and murd'ress, they proceed from you,

Shakespeare: "'Tis the eye of childhood / That fears a painted devil." [*Macbeth* 2.2.52–3, c. 1606]

As if a man should spit against the wind,
The filth returns in's face.

Yver: "Thou shalt be like him that spitteth against the wind, whose slaver fleeth in his own face." [Jacques Yver, *A Courtlie Controversie of Cupids Cautels*, tr. H. W., 1578]

(Dent 1960: 10–11)

Dent analysed *The White Devil* in detail (1960: 69–173), and concluded that 'the extent of Webster's borrowings was extraordinary even for the age in which we wrote' (1960: 9). He suggested that Webster must have used 'a commonplace book, in one part of which quotations were arranged by author rather than topic', and that the playwright must have had this book to hand as he wrote (1960: 16).

Webster's heavy use of non-original material should not be under-stood as unthinking plagiarism or as artistic laziness, however. As John Russell Brown has argued, Webster's 'restless mind was constantly leading him to repeat and modify what he had written', and his compilations 'were not likely to be thoughtless' (1977: xli). M. C. Bradbrook defends Webster's borrowing, citing modern authors like T. S. Eliot and James Joyce as having done something similar. She prefers the term 'bondings' to 'borrowings', suggesting that Webster uses his audience's familiarity with many of his sources to 'bond' particular cultural resonances or associations to the utterances of his characters (1980: 137–9). Thus, for example, when Cornelia quotes from *King Lear* as she weeps over the corpse of her son in V.ii, or from Ophelia in *Hamlet* as she goes mad in V.iv, the audience hear two voices at once: their memories of the earlier plays inflect the meanings they make of this one. In her grief and subsequent madness, Cornelia borrows the tragic stature of the earlier Shakespearean characters.

It may be that the characters themselves are 'borrowing' their words. Characters like Cornelia recite a wide range of what would have been recognizable proverbs and commonplaces, and as Richard Allen Cave argues, this may have given the effect 'of a character's seeking comfort and security in proverbial wisdom which the audience with its greater awareness of the play's action knows to be cruel illusion' (1988: 13). Dent notes that Flamineo's speeches in I.ii are drawn mainly from the French philosopher Michel de Montaigne, allowing the character 'to affect a nonchalance in evil he thinks a sign of sophistication, and to pretend (in vain) an easy familiarity with Bracciano as of two men of the world conversing with one another' (1960: 29).

Webster's key sources for *The White Devil* were accounts of the life and death of the historical Vittoria Accoramboni (1557–85), on whom his own fictional Vittoria is based. These accounts are the subject of another exhaustive study, Gunnar Boklund's *The Sources of The White Devil* (1966). Boklund surveys in minute detail the numerous docu-ments referring to Accoramboni's murder, concluding that Webster must have drawn from sources including Desiderius Erasmus's 1526 dialogue *Funus* ('The Funeral'), Pierre Boaistuau's philosophical treatise *Theatrum mundi* ('The Theatre or Rule of the World') and the English translation by John Florio of *A Letter Lately Written from Rome* (1966: 122). He notes that it is 'beyond reasonable doubt' that the version of Vittoria Accoramboni's life contained in a newsletter published by the Fugger banking house of Germany 'served Webster as a source for his play, although by no means necessarily or even probably in the form with which we are now familiar' (1966: 122). Indeed, Webster is highly unlikely to have had access to the German version, and probably consulted a now-lost English translation of an also lost Italian original.

However he came by it, the Fugger newsletter is clearly the source for much of Webster's plot. What makes it essential reading for the student of *The White Devil*, though, is what Webster adds to it. David Gunby, David Carnegie and Antony Hammond list Webster's key inventions, which include Vittoria's recounting of her 'dream' as a means of manipulating Bracciano into murdering her husband, her trial and subsequent imprisonment in the 'house of convertites', the manner of Bracciano's death, Marcello's murder, Cornelia's madness and of course the appearances of the ghosts (1995: 366–7). What is striking in the account below is that the historical Vittoria appears to have been entirely innocent – a far cry from the 'the famous Venetian Curtizan' of the play's title page, and indeed from the 'White Devil' of the title itself. Here, then, is the account from the Fugger newsletter in full:

The Murder of the Signora Accaramboni

New tidings of a pitiful act of murder that took place on the 22nd day of December of the new calendar in the year 1585, at Padua in Italy, a town belonging to the Venetian rulers.

The Duke Paolo Giordano Orsini, Duke of Bracciano, scion of one of the noblest Roman families had for wife the sister of the now reigning Grand Duke of Florence, with whom he had as issue of the marriage-bed a young Prince of the name of Giovanni. But as the said Duke had but little sexual intercourse with the former Duchess of Florence, he was induced by fleshly desire to break his marriage vows.

He conceived a burning passion for the wife of the nephew of the now reigning Pope Sixtus. But she did not wish to turn unfaithful to her husband, and therefore told him she was married and that no other man should approach her. Thereupon the said Duke forgot himself and had the husband of the lady (the nephew of the Pope) horribly murdered. He then once more approached the widow of the murdered man. But she curtly refused him because he was married and she a widow and not wishful to do such a thing. Thereupon the Duke Paolo Giordano forgot himself still further and had his own spouse, sister of the present Duke of Florence, put out of the way, in order to still his concupiscence for the above-named widow. Then, for the third time he paid his addresses to her. This time she made subjection to him but only on condition that he married her, which he did.

Meanwhile the Cardinal, the present Pope, did not rest in his desire to avenge the innocent blood of his nephew. But as he was not of much consideration, he has been placated. However, when he became Pope, the Duke wished to be reconciled with him. He knelt before him and begged for his blessing. Thereupon the Pope said: "Duke Paolo Giordano, you insulted the Cardinal Montalto: but Pope Sixtus pardons you. Do not come again, however, of that we warn you." The Duke was greatly alarmed at this speech and removed himself with his spouse to Padua, in Venetian territory, where he kept Court and had up to five hundred persons at his board. Nevertheless, before two months had passed, he died at Salo. Foul play was suspected. He left his spouse, who belonged to the noble Roman house of Accaramboni, a large property. The Grand Duke of Florence was by no means pleased with this testament, and took charge of the young forsaken Prince Giovanni, calling upon the widow at the same time to put aside the will. Should she marry again, he would deal handsomely by her: but he urged upon her to enter a convent or to remain a widow. Then also would he make handsome provision for her. But to this she would not agree, and wished to abide by the testament and to keep a retinue of one hundred persons. On the 22nd day of this month, at 2 o'clock at night, according to Italian time, her palace in Padua was found open. Fifty well-armed men thereupon entered and cruelly shot the brother of the Signora Accaramboni, a certain Duke Flaminio; as to the lady, they stabbed her where they found her at prayer. Although she pitifully entreated that she might be permitted first to conclude her orisons, the murderers fulfilled their deed. The most distinguished among them is Ludovico Orsini, the first chief of the Government here, cousin of the dead Paolo Giordano. Thereafter he entrenched himself with his assassins in his house. In the meanwhile the news was brought here and the Government has dispatched one of its Senators to Padua with authority to destroy the house of Orsini and to take the murderers alive or dead. The said Orsini surrendered himself with a dagger in his hand, and his house was fired upon from several large cannon. Thereby a number of his retainers perished, the remainder being taken prisoner.

From Venice, the 27th day of December 1585.

Yesternight the Government here decided that the Colonel Ludovico Orsini was to be strangled three hours after the delivery of their letter. His accomplices were to be dealt with according to their deserts. Without doubt they will be hanged and quartered.

The chief culprit Orsini confessed that he had perpetrated this murderous deed at the command of great personages. The students in Padua have armed themselves and cried out "Justice, Justice!"

From Venice, the 1st day of January 1586.

It has been recently reported that the Colonel of this Government, Ludovico Orsini, acted murderously and with his own hand slew in gruesome fashion the wife of the late Prince Paolo Giordano, Duke of Bracciano, and her brother, Duke Flaminio.

When the decision that he must die within three hours was made known to Ludovico Orsini, he confessed that although his years numbered but four-and-thirty, he had put to death with his own hands forty persons, believing that Justice would never lay hands upon him because he belonged to so illustrious a house. He had hoped likewise that he would not be publicly executed. But when he was informed that he was not to be strangled in a public place but in a chamber, he gave thanks for this judgment and penned two letters, one to his spouse and the other to the Government here. He commended to the latter's care his spouse and child, as well as his estate, so that they might not suffer on his account. He also made a will by which he bequeathed to the Government his armour, worth over and above six thousand crowns. The remainder of his property he left to his wife, who was at the time with child.

He gave fifty crowns to his executioner, in order that he might be dispatched quickly.

The brother of this Ludovico Orsini, Don Latino Orsini, is Governor of Candia under the Venetian rule. But shortly afterwards the Government sent a frigate to divest him of the command because they no longer put faith in him. And just as high as the house of Orsini had stood in esteem, as deep is now its fall.

After Ludovico Orsini had been strangled, his body was borne to the cathedral, the coffin decorated with tapestries and left lying there through the whole of this the 27th day of December. Then it was brought hither and interred in the Church of the Madonna dell' Orto, where Don Giordano and Don Valerio Orsini, the forbears of Ludovico, also lie buried.

The murdered Signora Accaramboni was a woman of great eloquence for as Ludovico Orsini was about to murder her, she was at prayer, and when the murderer said to her: "Do you recognize me?" she made answer "Yea, now it is time to prepare my soul. I beg of you by the Mercy of our Lord Jesus Christ, to let me make my confession and then do with me as you please." "Nay," answered the enemy, "now is not the time for confession."

In Padua near on six hundred burghers paraded in arms and cried "Justice, Justice!" Now follows the list of those who were publicly executed: Count Paganello Ubaldi and Captain Splandiano da Fermo. These two were the servants of the murdered lady, who did open her dwelling — the palace — and who were accomplices in the bloody deed. They were riven asunder with red-hot tongs, and killed with a hammer and then quartered. Buglion and Furio Savognano, two noblemen and secret advisers of Ludovico Orsini, have been secretly strangled.

Agrippa Tartaro de Monte Falco, the Comte de Camerion and thirteen more, some of them nobles, others arrant scoundrels, were all hanged.

Colonel Lorenzo Nobile del Borgo, Liverotto, and da Fermo were torn to pieces by the mob as they were firing upon the house. Twenty of the people lie imprisoned. They also will probably be hanged. (From von Klarwill 1926: 86–9)

Renaissance Italy on the Jacobean stage

Italian settings were immensely popular on the Jacobean stage. As noted above, Vittoria is described on *The White Devil*'s title page as a 'famous Venetian Curtizan', despite being neither a courtesan nor from Venice. The tagline, however, allows Webster to signal to his audience that his play is concerned with sexual and political intrigue; Italy, and especially Venice, was particularly associated with both. The Elizabethan scholar Roger Ascham wrote about his short stay in Venice in *The Schoolmaster* (1570): 'I thank God my abode there was but nine days. And yet I saw in that little time, in one city, more liberty to sin than I ever heard tell of in our noble city of London in nine years.' The stereotype was just as ingrained when Webster wrote his play; the travel writer Thomas Coryat noted in 1611 that 'the name of a Cortezan of Venice is famoused over all Christendom' (*Coryat's Crudities*).

But it was not just Italy's salacious sexual associations which interested the Jacobeans. Italian settings were also frequently symbolic of the murky world of politics, in which the rich and powerful plotted against, lied to, betrayed and murdered one another. The Catholic Church was depicted as particularly corrupt – England had, after all, been Protestant since the reign of Elizabeth I, and Catholics were viewed with extreme suspicion.

A focal point for this simultaneous fascination and mistrust was the Italian philosopher Niccolò Machiavelli (1469–1527), whose works had been translated into English and read widely. His most influential book was *The Prince* (1513), a treatise on the effective exertion of power which advocated the use of deception, force and betrayal when politically expedient. In England, Machiavelli was popularly seen as an evil influence; in 1552, for example, Ascham condemned those who 'with consciences confirmed with Machiavelle's doctrine ... think, say or do whatsoever may serve best for profit or pleasure' (*A Report and Discourse*).

On the stage, the 'machiavel' became a recognizable type. Marlowe's *The Jew of Malta* has 'Machevill' (the spelling of the name tellingly collided with the word 'evil') deliver a prologue in which he declares 'religion but a childish toy' (l. 14) and asserts the primacy of 'might' over law (l. 20). Shakespeare's Richard of Gloucester, meanwhile, declares that 'I can smile, and murder whiles I smile, ... And set the murderous Machiavel to school' (*3 Henry VI*, III.ii.182–93). Webster has Flamineo refer to Francisco as a 'Machivillain' (with a pun on 'villain') at V.iii.194, and the play's many references to 'policy' and 'politicians' can be understood as a sustained critique of unethical Machiavellian *realpolitik*. Indeed, Gasparo's remark that 'Princes give rewards with their own hands, / But death or punishment by the hands of others' (V.vi.188–9) directly echoes a recommendation of Machiavelli's in Chapter 9 of *The Prince*, while Vittoria's dying recognition that most people are duped by 'report' of great men's morality is strongly reminiscent of Machiavelli's observation of princes, cited in the excerpt below, that 'Every one sees what you appear to be, few really know what you are'.

It should be noted, though, that the popular characterizations of Machiavelli as an amoral opportunist are perhaps somewhat wide of the mark. Far from advising a small political elite in secret, Machiavelli published his reflections on power for all to read. Jonathan Dollimore, paraphrasing Antonio Gramsci, argues: 'In fact, far from telling the rulers how to be more effectively tyrannical, Machiavelli was revealing to "those who are not in the know" the truth about how tyranny operates, especially at the level of ideological legitimation' (2010: 22). Machiavelli had a serious influence on political thinking in England, leading thinkers such as Francis Bacon to observe 'that nature, nor the engagement of words, are not so forcible as custom', and that men behave 'as if they were dead images and engines moved only by the wheels of custom' (1972: 119). It is an idea about power and ideology which has potentially radical implications, and one which would not be out of place in the mouth of Flamineo.

Here is an excerpt from *The Prince*, in which the reader might detect some of the behaviours exhibited by several key characters in *The White Devil* (see, for example, Vittoria's speech at I.ii.230–56; Bracciano and Flamineo's orchestration of the murders in II.i and II.ii; and especially Francisco and Monticelso's shady private dealings at II.i.323–93, III.i.1–10, IV.i.1–97, and IV.ii.47–153):

Every one admits how praiseworthy it is in a prince to keep faith, and to live with integrity and not with craft. Nevertheless our experience has been that those princes who have done great things have held good faith of little account, and have known how to circumvent the intellect of men by craft, and in the end have overcome those who have relied on their word. [...] Therefore a wise lord cannot, nor ought he to, keep faith when such observance may be turned against him, and when the reasons that caused him to pledge it exist no longer. If men were entirely good this precept would not hold, but because they are bad, and will not keep faith with you, you too are not bound to observe it with them. Nor will there ever be wanting to a prince legitimate reasons to excuse this nonobservance. Of this endless modern examples could be given, showing how many treaties and engagements have been made void and of no effect through the faithlessness of princes; and he who has known best how to employ the fox has succeeded best.

But it is necessary to know well how to disguise this characteristic, and to be a great pretender and dissembler; and men are so simple, and so subject to present necessities, that he who seeks to deceive will always find someone who will allow himself to be deceived. [...]

Therefore it is unnecessary for a prince to have all the good qualities I have enumerated, but it is very necessary to appear to have them. And I shall dare to say this also, that to have them and always to observe them is injurious, and that to appear to have them is useful; to appear merciful, faithful, humane, religious, upright, and to be so, but with a mind so framed that should you require not to be so, you may be able and know how to change to the opposite.

And you have to understand this, that a prince, especially a new one, cannot observe all those things for which men are esteemed, being often forced, in order to maintain the state, to act contrary to faith, friendship, humanity, and religion. Therefore it is necessary for him to have a mind ready to turn itself accordingly as the winds and variations of fortune force it, yet, as I have said above, not to diverge from the good if he can avoid doing so, but, if compelled, then to know how to set about it.

For this reason a prince ought to take care that he never lets anything slip from his lips that is not replete with the above-named five qualities, that he may appear to him who sees and hears him altogether merciful, faithful, humane, upright, and religious. There is nothing more necessary to appear to have than this last quality, inasmuch as men judge generally more by the eye than by the hand, because it belongs to everybody to see you, to few to come in touch with you. Every one sees what you appear to be, few really know what you are, and those few dare not oppose themselves to the opinion of the many, who have the majesty of the state to defend them; and in the actions of all men, and especially of princes, which it is not prudent to challenge, one judges by the result.

For that reason, let a prince have the credit of conquering and holding his state, the means will always be considered honest, and he will be praised by everybody because the vulgar are always taken by what a thing seems to be and by what comes of it; and in the world there are only the vulgar, for the few find a place there only when the many have no ground to rest on. (Machiavelli, *The Prince*, Chapter 18: 'Concerning The Way In Which Princes Should Keep Faith', quoted in Marriott 1908: 141–5)

Power and politics in Jacobean England

Jacobean depictions of corrupt and decadent Italian courts were not simply criticisms of a far-off culture on the other side of Europe: many were thinly veiled portraits of an aristocratic world much closer to home. The court of James I had, by 1612, developed a reputation as a hotbed of vice and favouritism, and the King himself was renowned for his extravagance. Sir John Harington complained of a court masque in 1606 that he 'ne'er did see such lack of good order, discretion, and sobriety'.

The events which were to cement the Jacobean court's scandalous reputation occurred between 1613 and 1616. Sir Thomas Overbury was the secretary and close adviser to Sir Robert Carr, James's favourite at court. Carr began a liaison with Frances Howard, the married Countess of Essex; this led to her high-profile divorce from Essex and re-marriage to Carr in December 1613. Overbury, however, opposed the match – and this led to his rapid demise. He fell out of favour with the King (due in part, no doubt, to the fall-out from the divorce scandal) and refused an ambassadorial commission from him in April 1613; he was subsequently imprisoned in the Tower of London, where he died months later of a mysterious illness.

Rumours of foul play began to circulate, culminating in 1615 in the disclosure by the governor of the Tower, Sir Gervase Elwes, that he had caught Overbury's keeper Robert Weston bringing the prisoner poisoned food. Weston was put on trial, and refused to plead until he was finally threatened with *piene forte et dure* (being pressed to death with weights); found guilty, he was then put to death. Frances's servant Anne Turner was then tried, as was Sir Gervase Elwes himself, and both were sentenced to death and executed. Finally, Carr and his wife were tried and found guilty, but their lives were spared at the King's intervention. The episode was widely condemned as an example of gross injustice, and of the abuse of power and influence. At the scaffold, both Turner and Elwes denounced the court; Turner accused the majority of courtiers of 'malice, pride, whoredom, swearing and rejoicing in the fall of others' (see Briggs 1997: 237).

Though all this occurred *after* Webster had written *The White Devil*, the similarities are striking. Like Overbury, Flamineo is a secretary to a 'great man', having to act as a go-between in his master's adulterous affair. Like Vittoria, Frances Howard was widely and openly condemned as a 'whore' in a very public trial. The main victims in *The White Devil*, as in the Overbury affair, are the accessories, accomplices and tool-villains, while the truly powerful escape punishment. Finally, like Turner and Elwes, Webster's characters speak out against the court: Flamineo describes it as having made him 'more courteous, more lecherous by far' (I.ii.327), while Vittoria condemns it with her final words (V.vi.261–2; see also Antonio's last words in *The Duchess of Malfi*, V.iv.75). Interestingly, Webster probably knew Overbury personally. Webster dedicated *A Monumental Column* to Carr in 1612, and in 1615, he contributed to *Characters*, a collection of vivid descriptions of contemporary character types, which was posthumously attributed to Overbury.

There is at least one line in *The White Devil* which seems to be a direct reference to King James's actions. When in 1610 James's cousin Lady Arbella Stuart married William Seymour without having first sought the King's permission, James had her imprisoned in the Tower of London. This would surely have been fresh in the audience's memories as they heard Flamineo speak the following lines in the play:

> Verily, master courtier, extremity is not to be used in all offices. Say that a gentlewoman were taken out of her bed about midnight, and committed to Castle Angelo, to the tower yonder, with nothing about her, but her smock; would it not show a cruel part in the gentleman porter to lay claim to her upper garment, pull it o'er her head and ears, and put her in naked? (V.iv.39–45)

In temporarily collapsing the distance between the fictional Italian court and the real Jacobean one, Webster makes a direct link between Vittoria's abuse as a political pawn and Lady Arbella Stuart's.

Women and misogyny

At the end of Act II of Shakespeare's *Cymbeline*, the character Posthumus Leonatus delivers a violently misogynistic tirade:

> ... there's no motion
> That tends to vice in man but I affirm
> It is the woman's part; be it lying, note it,
> The woman's; flattering, hers; deceiving, hers;
> Lust and rank thoughts, hers, hers; revenges, hers;
> Ambitions, covetings, change of prides, disdain,
> Nice longing, slanders, mutability,
> All faults that may be named, nay, that hell knows,
> Why, hers in part or all. (II.v.20–8)

The audience are not necessarily encouraged to share his view – he has been deceived into thinking that his wife has been unfaithful, and on that basis alone the Jacobean audience must have seen his judgement as questionable. The speech does, however, give expression to a set of ideas about women which were disturbingly common during the period.

The idea that women were inherently sinful had its roots in the first book of the Bible. The book of Genesis tells the story of Adam and Eve in the Garden of Eden: God commands Adam not to eat the fruit of 'the tree of the knowledge of good and evil', but Eve is persuaded to violate God's command by a serpent, and she in turn tempts Adam. God, angry at her disobedience, devises a punishment: 'Unto the woman he said, I will greatly multiply thy sorrow and thy conception. In sorrow thou shalt bring forth children: and thy desire shall be to thy husband, and he shall rule over thee' (*King James Bible*, Genesis 3:16). The story was used in early modern culture, as Dympna Callaghan argues, as 'both the justification and the cause of woman's subjugation' (1989: 101). As an example, she cites the Elizabethan text *The Praise and Dispraise of Women* (1569), in which the author observes that 'Eve did first transgress, whose fault brought us in thrall' (1989: 101). Women, according to this standpoint, were responsible for sin itself, and therefore deserved everything they got.

Women had a clear hierarchical position in seventeenth-century England: they were subordinate to men. An advice book titled *A Godly Form of Household Government* (1598) describes it as 'a monstrous matter...for the wife to rebel against the husband', suggesting that a disobedient wife is like a body refusing to obey its own head. A passage from William Painter's book *The Palace of Pleasure* (1567) – a collection of classical and Italian tales which was widely used by Elizabethan dramatists, including Webster himself – makes it clear that women were expected to be submissive and deferential without exception:

> ...a woman being as it were the image of sweetness, courtesy and shame-fastness, so soon as she steppeth out of the right tract, and leaveth the smell of her duty and modesty, besides the denigration of her honour, thrusteth herself into infinite troubles and causeth the ruin of such which should be honoured and praised, if women's allurement solicited them not to folly.

The early modern woman, notes Lisa Jardine, thus 'has no means of escape: any single act which does not square with this emblem of passive and dutiful behaviour condemns the individual as "fallen" from the pedestal' (1983: 76).

During the Jacobean period, it was common for women to defend themselves in ecclesiastical courts from accusations of being a 'whore', just as Vittoria does in the play. In *Reading Shakespeare Historically*, Jardine surveys a number of court records from the period and notes the large number of cases 'in which individual women believed their reputations had been harmed by imputations of unchastity' (1996: 25). In her sample, she reports, '90 per cent of cases concerning a female plaintiff involved her sexual reputation' (1996: 26).

Women were defined primarily according to their relationships with men, whether as a daughter, as a wife, or as a widow. Again, the idea is central in the book of Genesis: God creates Eve by taking a rib from Adam, leading Adam to declare her 'bone of my bones, and flesh of my flesh' (Genesis 2:23). The independent, assertive woman was thus seen as an aberration: the 'masculine' woman, 'bold' in speech and 'impudent' in action, was described as 'most monstrous' in the anonymous pamphlet *Hic Mulier: or the Man-Woman* in 1620. Jardine notes that 'the drama of the early modern period is full of set-piece denunciations of the "not-woman" in her many forms', and she lists Webster's solo-authored plays as 'typical' examples (1983: 93–4). She notes that the archetype of Jacobean drama's demonized 'not woman' was Lady Macbeth (1983: 97–8), and it is significant that Vittoria borrows a famous line of this character's during her trial ('Terrify babes, my lord, with painted devils', III.ii.147, paraphrases Lady Macbeth's ''Tis the eye of childhood / That fears a painted devil', *Macbeth* II.ii.52–3).

Certainly Webster depicts a highly sexist and patriarchal world in *The White Devil*. Bracciano and Francisco dominate their respective dukedoms, and characters like Isabella are treated as symbolic bargaining tokens rather than as active individuals in their own rights. The play is skewed more towards a male perspective than a female one: male characters like Flamineo and Francisco are allowed long soliloquies in which they address the audience directly, whereas the female characters are not. It is important to remember that all the female characters would have been played, as was the custom on the Jacobean stage, by male actors (usually boys), and thus at a further remove from the reality of the audience's world than their male counterparts. The play also gives expression to misogynist ideas: Monticelso's invective against 'whores' in the trial scene (III.ii.78–101) is a memorable example, and Flamineo engages in sexist commentary throughout the play (notably at I.ii.17–25, IV.ii.149–85, and V.vi.154–66). A key theme throughout these diatribes is the deceitful and duplicitous nature of women, and it is an idea which the central plot of the play might be seen to support. Vittoria is, after all, repeatedly deceptive.

On the other hand, the fact that Webster *depicts* such a misogynistic world does not necessarily mean that he endorses its values. Indeed, he creates in Vittoria a strong and potentially sympathetic female character whose victimization at the hands of powerful men might provoke outrage and indignation in the audience. Certainly there were voices in Jacobean England – both male and female – which spoke out against the oppression and vilification of women. Either way, the play makes a resonant, if ambiguous, contribution to a debate which was very current at the time of its first performances.

A central forum in which this debate played out was the pamphlet war instigated in 1615 by the publication of *An Arraignment of Lewd, Idle, Froward, and Unconstant Women* by Joseph Swetnam. This document was an odd mix of jokes, historical anecdotes, biblical references and misogynistic invective aimed at a readership of 'the ordinary sort of giddy-headed young men'. In it, Swetnam denounced women in a variety of ways, condemning them as animalistic, dishonest, disloyal, deceptive and uncontrollable. The pamphlet provoked a number of anti-misogynist counter-responses, many of them by women: Rachel Speght's *Mouzell for Melastomus*, Ester Sowernam's *Ester Hath Hanged Haman*, and Constantia Munda's *The Worming of a Madde Dogge* were all printed in 1617, while the satirical play *Swetnam the Woman-Hater, Arraigned by Women* was published in 1620. The latter was performed at the Red Bull Theatre by the Queen Anne's Men – the same company and theatre that had staged *The White Devil* a few years earlier – and it features an almost direct inversion of Webster's trial scene, in which the woman-hating Swetnam (under the name 'Misogynos') is put on trial, and judged, by a 'female court'.

The excerpt below is from Swetnam's pamphlet. The reader might compare it with some of the misogynistic passages in *The White Devil*, in which characters express a similar mistrust of women's outward appearances and sexuality (see, for example, III.ii.78–101 and IV.ii.149–85):

> The Second Chapter showeth the manner of such Women as live upon evil report; it also showeth that the beauty of Women hath been the bane of many a man, for it hath overcome valiant and strong men, eloquent

and subtle men. And, in a word, it hath overcome all men, as by example following shall appear.

... Then who can but say that women sprung from the Devil? Whose heads, hands, and hearts, minds and souls are evil, for women are called the hook of all evil because men are taken by them as fish is taken with the hook.

For women have a thousand ways to entice thee and ten thousand ways to deceive thee and all such fools as are suitors unto them: some they keep inhand with promises, and some they feed with flattery, and some they delay with dalliances, and some they please with kisses. They lay out the folds of their hair to entangle men into their love; betwixt their breasts is the vale of destruction; and in their beds there is hell, sorrow and repentance. Eagles do not eat men till they are dead, but women devour them alive, for a woman will pick thy pocket and empty thy purse, laugh in thy face and cut thy throat. They are ungrateful, perjured, full of fraud, flouting and deceit, unconstant, waspish, toyish, light, sullen, proud, discourteous and cruel, and yet they were by God created, and by nature formed, and therefore by policy and wisdom to be avoided; for good things abused are to be refused. Or else for a month's pleasure, she may make thee go stark naked. She will give thee roast meat, but she will beat thee with the spit. If thou hast crowns in thy purse, she will be thy heart's gold until she leave thee not a whit of white money. They are like summer birds, for they will abide no storm, but flock about thee in the pride of thy glory, and fly from thee in the storms of affliction; for they aim more at thy wealth than at thy person, and esteem more thy money than any man's virtuous qualities. For they esteem of a man without money as a horse doth of a fair stable without meat. They are like Eagles which will always fly where the carrion is.

They will play the horse-leech to suck away thy wealth, but in the winter of thy misery, she will fly away from thee. Not unlike the swallow, which in the summer harboreth herself under the eaves of a house, and against winter flieth away, leaving nothing but dirt behind her. (Swetnam, *The Arraignment of Lewde, Idle, Froward, and Unconstant Women*, Chapter 2)

4 Key Performances and Productions

The White Devil on the modern stage

Until Cambridge University's Marlowe Dramatic Society staged *The White Devil* in 1920, there had been no productions of the play on record since the late seventeenth century. The 1920 production, performed by undergraduates, was enormously influential in re-igniting interest in the play as theatre; it was endorsed enthusiastically by both F. L. Lucas (later editor of Webster's *Complete Works*) and the novelist E. M. Forster. Forster, comparing the production very favourably with the work of professional London actors, described it as 'one of the best Elizabethan performances that we are likely to see for a long time' (*New Statesman*, 20 March 1920).

A number of short-lived revivals followed over the next two decades. The Renaissance Theatre staged just two performances at London's Scala Theatre in 1925, and in 1935 the Phoenix Society did a single performance at St Martin's Theatre in a bid to revive the society. The Marlowe Society restaged the play at Cambridge in 1931 under the same director as its 1920 production, John Tresidder Sheppard, who was by this point Vice-Provost of King's College. Like the previous production, it made use of an all-male cast, none of whom were identified by name in the programme, and according to the review in *The Times*, 'use [was] made of the auditorium for the entrances and exits of many of the characters' (9 March 1931).

The twentieth century's first full-scale professional run of the play was not mounted until after the war. Michael Benthall directed a production for the Duchess Theatre in 1947, starring the famous actor and dancer Robert Helpmann as Flamineo. *The Times* noted:

> Only a few years ago, it would have been considered a fantastic risk to bring *The White Devil* to the public stage for an unlimited run. There is some risk still, but it has lessened almost out of recognition, for there has grown up in the meanwhile a generation which has learned to approach the work of the old masters of the English theatre with hopeful, open-eyed curiosity. (7 March 1947)

A number of radio broadcasts over the next few years secured the play's position in the classical repertoire: the BBC produced the play in 1948, 1955, 1960 and 1969 – though the last of these broadcasts inspired critic David Wade to complain that the play sounded 'the most entire nonsense' (*The Times*, 8 November 1969).

This rehabilitation of *The White Devil* soon extended to America, where the play was staged for one night only at New York's Phoenix Theatre by Jack Landau in 1955. This modern-dress production was the first of many which likened the play to a 'gangster world'; Landau argued in an article for *Theatre Arts* that Webster's characters 'live in what might be called an Elizabethan Mickey Spillane world' (Holdsworth 1984: 234). Landau put *The Duchess of Malfi* in a similar setting in 1957, and remounted his *White Devil* for a major revival at the Circle in the Square, New York, in 1965. The gangland setting was used again by Michael Blakemore at the Guthrie Theatre, Minneapolis, in 1977 – an attempt, argues David Carnegie, 'to establish political and social relevance for a modern audience' and 'to find an American imaginative equivalent to the Jacobean English version of Italy' (1995: 113).

There was a spate of productions in Britain in the late 1960s. Richard Eyre directed the play for Edinburgh's Royal Lyceum in 1968, while the following year saw productions at Liverpool's Everyman Theatre (directed by John Russell Brown), the Stables Company, Manchester and London's Old Vic. The latter was a collaboration between director Frank Dunlop and designer Piero Gherardi for the National Theatre Company, and was somewhat experimental in nature: Gherardi, famous for his work with the *avant-garde* film director Federico Fellini, designed a large symbolic set which resembled an enormous wall, each brick of which was several feet across. Benedict Nightingale described it in the *New Statesman* as 'a wall as it might be perceived by insects or small reptiles: toads, perhaps, or grasshoppers or drones' (21 November 1969). Thus, each of the characters was clothed in an insect-like costume, with enormous, wing-like, lacy ruffs and elaborately-styled hair. In a programme note, Dunlop cited a 1916 assessment of the play by the poet Rupert Brooke as key influence; a play of Webster's, Brooke had noted, was 'full of the feverish and ghastly turmoil of a nest of maggots':

> Maggots are what the inhabitants of this universe most suggest and resemble. The sight of their fever is only alleviated by the permanent calm, unfriendly summits and darknesses of the background of death and doom. For that is equally a part of Webster's universe. Human beings are writhing grubs in an immense night. (1916: 158)

The production's highly symbolic and non-psychological style was, for Richard Allen Cave at least, ultimately a weakness: the design turned Geraldine McEwan's Vittoria into 'a she-devil, a threatening basilisk', while 'most of the other performers seemed dwarfed by the costumes and production-effects' (1988: 44, 50). 'By seeing *The White Devil* as a vehicle for an exhibition of high camp,' concludes Cave, 'Frank Dunlop robbed a potentially fine cast of the chance to explore Webster's psychological artistry' (1988: 53).

Cave much preferred the Old Vic's second production of the play – an adaptation by Edward Bond, directed by Michael Lindsay-Hogg in 1976. Lindsay-Hogg set the play in an Art Deco hotel, and its characters became latter-day politicians and celebrities. Quite unlike Geraldine McEwan's villainous Vittoria, Glenda Jackson presented the character as a sympathetic, intelligent woman; 'you could sense her mind outstripping Monticelso's at the trial,' reports Cave, 'and grimly apprehending its inevitable conclusion long before the Cardinal actually succumbed to malice' (1988: 54). By inspiring sympathy where Dunlop's interpretation had previously encouraged critical judgement, the 1976 production was, as Christina Luckyj notes, 'a direct response to – even a challenge to – the earlier one' (2008: xxvi).

Staging *The White Devil* today: four case studies

The rest of this chapter will examine, in detail, four mainstream theatre productions of *The White Devil*. These will not be dealt with production-by-production, but rather topic-by-topic – the suggestion being that this chapter should be useful not merely as a stage history, but as a series of topics for practical consideration when staging the play. The productions under examination are those directed by Philip Prowse for the National Theatre in 1991, by Gale Edwards for the Royal Shakespeare Company in 1996, by Philip Franks for the Lyric Hammersmith in 2000 and by Jonathan Munby for the Menier Chocolate Factory in 2008. Franks and Munby both recorded interviews specifically for this book, and these are quoted below.

Philip Prowse, the director of the National Theatre production, had already established a long association with the play by 1991. A visual artist by training (he studied at the Slade School of Fine Art), he had designed a production for the Glasgow Citizens Theatre in 1971, setting the play in a 'sinister half-lit world of anonymous black-robed courtiers, with a central pit down which fell the dead and from which rose the ghosts' (Carnegie 1995: 111). He worked on the play again at the Citizens in 1978, as the designer for *Painter's Palace of Pleasure*, an amalgamation of *'Tis Pity She's a Whore*, *The Duchess of Malfi* and *The White Devil*. He then both directed and designed the play at the Greenwich Theatre in 1984, in a production which was once again dominated by candles and cowls. His *Duchess of Malfi* at the National Theatre in 1985 drew widespread attention, with a stellar cast including Ian McKellen, Eleanor Bron, Jonathan Hyde and Edward Petherbridge. The production of *The White Devil* which he directed and designed for the same theatre in 1991 can thus be seen as the culmination of a long affiliation with Webster's work.

Gale Edwards's production for the Royal Shakespeare Company in 1996 was the company's first ever staging of the play. Edwards, an Australian director, had made her name in Britain with productions of George Bernard Shaw's *Saint Joan* and Shakespeare's *The Taming of the Shrew*; the latter had successfully reclaimed Shakespeare's comedy for a post-feminist audience as a vibrant but misogynistic dream, and she had concluded the play with a new ending. She explained her reasons for choosing *The White Devil* as her next project to the *Independent*: 'I adore the language and the imagery, but most of all I love its flamboyant recklessness.... It feels like a roller-coaster ride or a ghost-train – you go for the thrills and spills along the way.' Discussing the play's 'passionate bloodlust and sexuality', she identified Webster's 'part seduction-enjoyment' and 'part revulsion' as a key source of fascination for her (*Independent*, 24 April 1996). She returned to the play for a similar production with the Sydney Theatre Company in 2000, but the discussion of her work in this chapter is based on her production for the RSC.

The third production under consideration here was directed by another seasoned Websterian, the actor and director Philip Franks. In his interview for this chapter, Franks admitted to having been 'preoccupied' by Webster since his undergraduate days at Oxford, when he played Bosola in a production of *The Duchess of Malfi*, and focused on the playwright for his long essay finals. He directed *The Duchess of Malfi* at the Greenwich Theatre in 1995, with a cast including Juliet Stevenson and Simon Russell Beale – but, feeling that he had been 'too timid with the play', he returned to it in 2006 at the West Yorkshire Playhouse for what he felt was 'a much better production' with Imogen Stubbs in the title role. This, he says, 'was largely because in the intervening years I'd had a look at *The White Devil.*' Franks's *The White Devil* was staged in 2000, a result of the desire of the Lyric Hammersmith's artistic director Neil Bartlett to produce a 'big Jacobean play' (interview).

The fourth and most recent case study – Jonathan Munby's production for the Menier Chocolate Factory – was the result of a specific brief from the theatre's artistic director, David Babani, to stage a revenge tragedy. Munby, who had a background in directing classical work for such companies as the RSC and Shakespeare's Globe, was immediately attracted to *The White Devil* – not only because it offered 'some really interesting points of discussion and provocation', but also because it was, he felt, particularly well suited to the intimacy of the Menier space:

> We wanted to create moments of thrilling theatricality and spectacle within the Chocolate Factory. Given that the space is actually quite small, we could actually get the audience inside the drama, and therefore inside the horror. I think Webster takes the stage violence to a different level – more so than Shakespeare, more so even than Ford. It's almost pornographic. It's extremely voyeuristic – he places the spectator in an interesting relation to these acts of violence. (Interview)

The production went on to be nominated for the *What's On Stage* Theatregoers' Choice award for Best Off-West End Production.

Concept and design

One of the first questions faced by a director and designer in staging any play is where they wish to set it. This is perhaps even more important in classical theatre, where it has become common to set plays in often radically different locations and historical periods from those suggested in the text. Setting and design are almost always predicated upon particular readings or interpretations of the play, and stage design, whether overtly or implicitly, asks its audience to make the same imaginative connections themselves.

In Philip Prowse's production, the design was arguably the focus (Prowse is, as noted above, a distinguished visual artist as well as a director). The action took place in a cavernous, vault-like edifice, walled with brickwork, suggesting either a cathedral or a gigantic mausoleum. Huge slabs engraved in Latin were spread across the floor, many of them broken and piled up, and an altar-like structure stood in the middle, surrounded by black tombs. Hanging from the ceiling on an enormous chain was a large golden ball, which gave the impression (given its surroundings) of a wrecking ball in the process of demolition. Reviews in *The Times* (19 June 1991), the *Independent* (20 June 1991) and the *Guardian* (20 June 1991) all noted that the set's connotations of death, burial and catastrophe recalled T. S. Eliot's observation that 'Webster was much possessed by death / And saw the skull beneath the skin'.

The costumes, too, drew attention to the production's symbolism of ritual and death. The play's world was populated by a large number of hooded figures with ragged crucifixes stitched onto their cowls. Like the set, the costumes were dominated by the colours black and gold, with most characters' costumes moving increasingly towards total blackness over the course of the performance. There were some notable exceptions, however: Monticelso graduated from a completely red costume to an entirely white one upon his accession to Pope, and the colour symbolism linking him with the play's title was foregrounded all the more by the fact that those around him were by this point wearing very dark colours. Vittoria, meanwhile, spent most of the production barefoot, implying an earthy sensuality, and wore a luxurious gold dress, not a white one, for her wedding. If this would seem to suggest a brazen and mercenary Vittoria, though, this was undercut by the final scene, in which both she and Flamineo were dressed in white as their killers wore black.

The critical response to this emphatically design-led production was largely negative. Emrys Jones felt that while it was 'visually impressive', the actors were 'overwhelmed by the setting' (*Times Literary Supplement*, 28 June 1991). John Peter agreed, arguing that 'it subordinates dramatic clarity to lordly visual flamboyance' (*Sunday Times*, 23 June 1991), while Michael Billington suggested that the production was more pictorial than dramatic: 'If you froze the action at any point, you would have a stunning picture. But it remains a fundamentally static piece' (*Guardian*, 20 June 1991). Prowse himself had perhaps anticipated such a response, in fact, criticizing the 'puritanism in the British theatre which resists visual literacy' in an interview before the production had even opened: 'If you have been brought up blind, as people tend to be in this country, then it is very hard to know how to handle visual imagery. So people don't know how to respond' (*Sunday Times*, 2 June 1991). For him, the visual aesthetic of the production was far more important than the text of the play; as he put it in another interview, in his view 'the author's words are no more important than the work of the usherettes' (*Daily Telegraph*, 20 June 1991). Gabrielle Dawes, herself a National Theatre usherette, wrote in response that she felt Prowse had disregarded the text 'to the point that no one can understand a single aspect of the plot' (*Independent*, 22 June 1991).

Gale Edwards's production for the RSC was praised by Michael Billington for having avoided the same pitfall. 'You emerge,' he noted, 'discussing the play rather than arguing about the concept' (*Guardian*, 29 April 1996). This should not be read, however, as a suggestion that this production had somehow allowed its audience unhampered access to a 'pure' version of Webster's text – such a feat is impossible in the theatre, in which decisions and interpretations are made at every turn. Rather, Edwards had created, with her designer Peter J. Davison, a setting for the play in which all the design elements helped to tell a coherent and compelling story.

A key feature of the design was a square trapdoor, covered by a metal grate, which stood in the centre of the playing space. In an article on the production, Nick Tippler describes it as a 'fatal pivot between this limbo and ultimate damnation' (2000: 276), and much of the action which took place in and upon it was highly significant: it was the site of most of the play's murders, with some of the victims' bodies sinking into it afterwards; the grieving Cornelia rose up from it before descending back into it with Marcello's corpse in V.iv; Bracciano's dying ravings were delivered from it, and his murder staged upon it. Complementing this centrepiece at the bottom of the stage was another at the top: a huge portrait of actor Ray Fearon as Bracciano which hung high above the stage. This portrait remained in place – signifying, perhaps, the character's dominance over the play's events – until the moment of his death. Here, as Bracciano succumbed to his macabre hallucinations below, the picture was ripped away, revealing in its frame a collection of skulls and bones. The review in *The Times* once again linked this moment to the famous Eliot poem (9 January 1997).

The design also split off the back of the playing space with a row of pillars. This separated space provided a site for the many passages which require unobserved characters to overhear the conversations of others: Bracciano, Camillo, Vittoria, Zanche and Cornelia all used it during I.ii, for example, and many of the furtive conversations between characters not wishing to be overheard took place within it. It became dominated by Flamineo in the second half of the play, making a clear visual statement about the character's position within the world of the play: detached, isolated and always observing. Interestingly, Francisco also began to use it much more frequently in Act V.

Colour symbolism was once again in evidence. The Tudor-style costumes were mostly dark, often made from leather. Vittoria and Zanche wore reds and oranges and had their cleavages exposed; Isabella, meanwhile, wore a steely blue, creating a marked disparity between the play's central female characters (one might argue that the production was playing, here, into the female stereotypes discussed in Chapter 3). Coloured lighting was used extensively to point up key contrasts, alternating between red for the hot, luxurious world of Bracciano and Vittoria (in I.ii, V.i and V.ii, for example), and blue for the icy political scenes dominated by Francisco and Monticelso (most of Acts III and IV). The trial scene split the stage between a blue wash and a red spotlight (in which Vittoria stood, of course), and the blue light made Monticelso, in his Cardinal's red, conspicuous, linking him visually with Vittoria's sensuality. When he became Pope, Monticelso not only remained in a red costume, but stood upon a huge red cloth which stretched from the floor to the ceiling. As Lodovico resolved to revenge, he too stepped onto the red cloth, symbolically implying that despite Monticelso's spoken opposition to the plan, the new Pope's unspoken desire was far less wholesome. Finally, the production made extensive use of backlighting, so that characters like Flamineo and Francisco cast huge shadows downstage as they delivered their soliloquies (and, in the latter case, as Bracciano died). These shadows were, of course, loaded with metaphorical meaning – not least of which was the suggestion that these two characters were bringers of death, and consumed by evil.

The concept and design for Philip Franks's production at the Lyric Hammersmith in 2000 was a direct response to Philip Prowse's heavily stylized staging at the National. 'I didn't want monks' habits and tolling bells,' says Franks. 'I wanted a vibrant world, one that's lit by fire and neon, one that's hot and dangerous.' For this reason, Franks chose to set the play in the 1950s Rome of Fellini's *La Dolce Vita*:

> You have to find an equivalent society which is just out of reach, enough for it to be a story, but near enough to be resonant, just as Renaissance Italy was for Jacobean England. So you find the equivalent. And the world of early Fellini is a very, very useful one, because it deals with people who are obsessed with sex, fashion, violence, and a kind of empty life, as it were, posing on the ruins of a destroyed society (and particularly Catholic society) which is seen to be corrupt and falling to bits. (Interview)

Reviewers certainly picked up on this connection, with Brian Logan noting the period's 'sharp suits and decadence', and 'women throwing off the yoke of patriarchy and the Catholic Church' (*Independent*, 17 September 2000). For Lyn Gardner, though, the specific modern setting was an implausible one: 'it stretches credulity,' she complained, 'to accept the level of church and papal corruption that the text demands' (*Guardian*, 16 September 2000).

Franks also made use of a very modern idiom in order to reclaim the play as a psychological one. 'I really didn't want it to be about great big over-made-up grotesques,' he explains; 'I wanted it to be about real people fighting for their lives.' The violence, he says, 'was as real as we could make it. It wasn't emblematic – it was painful, and ugly, and sad.' For Franks, Webster's presentation of underhand dealing, violent revenge and its consequences 'has a huge amount in common with *The Sopranos* and with the *Godfather* trilogy' (interview). Thus, the male characters wore sleek black suits and carried guns, tapping into the visual iconography of twentieth-century gangster films. At least one critic noted the influence: 'the continuing popularity of the Italian gangster genre taps into the same relish for shamelessly bad behaviour that Webster so colourfully exploited,' wrote Charles Isherwood in his review of the production (*Variety*, 23 September 2000).

A 'great deal of the way the production developed,' says Franks, came from his collaboration with its designer Rae Smith (interview). Smith's set drew these various influences together into a single symbolic image. Based on a photograph of a catwalk model show in Milan, it was composed of a suspended white platform and some precarious walkways, floating above a huge heap of rubbish and rubble comprised of old church pews, masonry and even a statue of the Madonna. The connotations of the decaying Catholic world were obvious, and the notion of the catwalk was, explains Franks, 'that this world is a very, very unsafe one, and that if you fall off it, you might not be able to get back on it again'. Nailed to the back wall of the stage was a large sword, which was used to represent both the sword of justice (in the trial, for example), and the crucifix (in the house of convertites). 'Not for the first time and not for the last,' says Franks, 'it was a crucifix made of a violent instrument' (interview).

Jonathan Munby's production sprung from a similar conceptual starting-point to Franks's. Munby and his designer, Philip Whitcomb, wanted to create what he describes as 'a parallel universe':

> It was about suggesting that the actions of the play, and indeed some of the views in the play, were not just 400 years old, but actually contemporary and living. [...] So we wanted to find a way of giving it a contemporary context that looked and felt recognizable, but that was its own world. It's still a world of knives, rather than guns. It's still a world where the Catholic Church has the power that it would have had 400 years ago in Europe. So it wasn't Italy 2008, but our own Italy, in a contemporary context that felt recognizable. (Interview)

The costumes, then, were largely modern ones, and the set very simple, allowing the audience to fill out the details with their own imaginations.

One of the most distinctive aspects of Munby's design concept was that the play was staged in traverse. Thus, the audience sat either side of a very narrow stage, facing one another over a corridor which was bookended by a set of gold doors at either end. For Munby, this was an opportunity to take the audience 'away from the safety of a proscenium' so that they were 'inside the drama and inside the room' with the characters. But the staging had a conceptual basis too, as Munby explains:

> There's so much opposition in the play – whether it's Vittoria versus the Cardinal, or Vittoria versus Bracciano. I thought how interesting it would be to place those characters, in terms of their opposition, on some kind of runway or performance space, that was built around that confrontation – and then to place the audience in opposition to each other. I liked the idea of us being able to view this drama in opposition to another audience member, to see and gauge their reaction, so that there was a dialogue between us, the audience, as we witnessed this specific dialogue between characters. (Interview)

In this sense, Vittoria – and, for that matter, all the other characters – were on trial for real, before an audience who were encouraged not only to reflect upon the action before them, but also upon one another's reactions.

Munby's production was designed to be a ritualistic 'theatre of cruelty' (interview). Not only was the space contained and claustrophobic: Munby was keen to generate a completely immersive theatrical event. Real incense was used, real candles flickered – the audience would even, at one point in the play, have caught the smell of real disinfectant. Music and lighting played important roles. 'I didn't want to shy away on any level from this being a very real and visceral experience,' says Munby. 'I always had Vittoria's line "O me, this place is hell" in my mind, and at times we wanted to be able to create that' (interview). Several of the reviews commented upon what Mark Shenton described as its 'frank and uncomfortable intimacy' (*Sunday Express*, 26 October 2008), and, as parts of the space became curtained off and candles and incense filled the gloom, this was intensified by the sense that the audience were, as Munby puts it, 'almost inside somebody's grave' (interview).

Finally, Munby's interpretation of the play was informed by a very real sense of topicality. Over the rehearsal period, he had encouraged his cast to collect newspaper clippings of stories of political hypocrisy and corruption – especially any relating to the Italian government or the Catholic Church. The Church had, in 2008, been rocked by a series of sexual abuse scandals, and Pope Benedict himself had been criticized for failing to take a hard enough stance against the alleged abusers. At the height of all this, photographs of the Pope had been widely circulated in the press showing the Pontiff wearing bright red designer shoes underneath his white robes. 'There was something about that as a kind of metaphorical image that struck me in terms of my investigation,' says Munby, drawing attention to its connotations of duplicity and corruption (interview). As a result, Monticelso wore a very similar costume in the final production, his red shoes below his white robes signifying his continued links with the criminal underworld.

Editing

The White Devil is just over 3000 lines long. Unedited, the text would take well over three hours to perform, so the majority of modern productions make substantial cuts to the play. Given its large number of characters, it is also generally practical for even the wealthiest of theatre companies to reduce the number of roles.

Cutting the play is not without its problems, but it also presents the person doing this work with a series of opportunities. Reorganizing the beginning or the end of the play will necessarily adjust the focus of the entire production, positioning a particular character or idea as central and discarding others as peripheral. Removing particular scenes and speeches can have the consequence of simplifying, obscuring or sometimes even clarifying a particular character's arc over the play, and may have the knock-on effect of repositioning another character as more worthy of the audience's sustained attention. In line with modern theatregoing conventions, most productions put an interval approximately halfway through the play, and it is usual for the first half to end on a 'cliff-hanger'; precisely where the interval is inserted, therefore, makes a number of inferences about where the audience should consider the play's central dramatic interest to lie.

Prowse's production made several key edits. Surprisingly, given Prowse's interest in the visual, spectacular scenes like the dumb-shows and the election of the Pope were under-emphasized. A striking visual element was added to I.i, however, in which a near-naked Lodovico (whose body bore signs of torture) was dragged onstage by two hooded guards. Zanche took the place of the Conjuror in II.ii, implying a greater complicity with Bracciano's actions than is usual for this character. Perhaps the production's most daring departure from the text, though, was Prowse's decision to have the corpse of Camillo (and, later, Isabella's) on stage for significant sections of the play. In his 1985 *Duchess of Malfi*, a personified figure of Death had 'literally walked amongst the characters', and Eleanor Bron's Duchess had joined him, following her murder, to become 'a ghostly witness of the action' (Cave 1988: 64, 66). Prowse repeated the motif in this production, with Monticelso revealing Camillo's corpse during the trial scene, and leaving it onstage until the end of IV.iii. After Lodovico's exit from this scene, Isabella's ghost (also played by Bron) re-entered, crossed Camillo's body, and kneeled; Camillo awoke, and the lights went to black for the interval. During the play's second half, both bodies were onstage, propped up against the altar. As Bracciano lay dying, Isabella stretched her hand towards him, and he, seeing her, cried out in terror. Clearly, for Prowse, the focus was on death and what might come afterwards.

Edwards's production edited the play in order to emphasize the two arcs of its narrative (see 'Assessments of the play's structure', Chapter 6). Opening with the image of Isabella kissing her husband's portrait, the production drew attention to an aspect of Isabella's devotion that is only mentioned in the text – the report that she performs this ritual 'nightly' (II.ii.25). The next appearance of the ritual – Isabella's murder during the dumb-show of II.ii – was then re-positioned so that it occurred later in the play. III.ii was split so that the scene depicting Isabella's death could occur *after* Vittoria's trial (III.ii.1–294), but naturally before Francisco's discovery of it (III.ii.295 onwards). This meant that until the end of the trial, the action of the play was focused solely on Camillo's murder and its consequences, with Isabella's death provoking the action of the second half.

Indeed, Francisco's discovery of his sister's murder occurred immediately after Bracciano had been informed of it, lending emphasis to the sinister hypocrisy of Bracciano's line 'Now you and I are friends, sir' (III.ii.295) and poignancy to his observation that 'You have lost too much already' (III.ii.300). Significantly, it also absolved Vittoria of any involvement whatsoever in Isabella's murder (aside, perhaps, from having inspired it).

The editing of Edwards's production also drew greater attention to the play's 'tool villains'. Ending the first half of the play with Flamineo's soliloquy at IV.ii.245–9 made this character's rise and fall one of the play's chief interests, and the staging of this speech – backlit and underscored with music – invested it with a kind of demonic significance. Lodovico, meanwhile, was characterized as the moral core of the play, the straight and honourable revenger. A light counterpart to the devilish Flamineo, Lodovico was at the centre of the production's almost identical opening and closing images, standing in a spotlight in the middle of the stage as a light shower rained down upon him. The opening image was of him gazing longingly up at Isabella as she kissed her husband's portrait; the closing one, of him as the sole surviving assassin, his revenge complete.

Franks's production made a similar interpretation of Lodovico, but achieved it though very different means, and de-emphasized the role. 'I cut Lodovico,' admits Franks, 'in order to make him into a different character':

> I cut all the banishment stuff, and made him Isabella's chauffeur, who was secretly in love with her – a bit like that film, *The Hireling*, with Robert Shaw and Sarah Miles – so that his revenge motive came absolutely from the love of a servant for a mistress. (Interview)

Having cut the whole of I.i, then, Franks opened the play with I.ii, in a staging which emphasized the debauched world of Bracciano and Vittoria. The first image was of a door opening out onto a hot Mediterranean patio, as Camillo, Vittoria and their drunken guests spilled out from a riotous party which had been going on indoors. Bracciano, their celebrity guest, was being shown out – but then, of course, he did not leave.

The editing of this production was geared towards positioning Vittoria as its protagonist, and Francisco as its villain. Thus, while the

second half opened with Vittoria's suffering in the house of convertites (IV.ii), the first half closed with the image of Francisco going
slowly mad. Having begun his long soliloquy (IV.i.74 onwards) calmly
and in complete control, he had, by the end, become thunderous. As
Rhoda Koenig's review describes it, actor Timothy Walker 'lightly
caresses the verse as he outlines his scheme for vengeance, and then,
still calmly, but devastatingly, snaps out his plan for Bracciano: to
"play at football with thy head"' (*Independent*, 19 September 2000).

Munby, meanwhile, framed his production so that it opened and
closed on a visual joke. Paul Taylor's review is perhaps the most
evocative description:

> At the start, as we take our seats, a functionary is seen in the final stages of
> mopping the marble floor of the Italian court. At the finish, he's back on
> with his cleaning equipment – only by now we can appreciate the neces-
> sity of his task as he swabs away the gore from the multiple deaths we have
> witnessed in between. (*Independent*, 15 October 2008)

Munby explains that the idea was to illustrate, with a touch of
humour, that such tales of bloody revenge 'are cyclical and universal',
and that this was 'a country able to simply wipe the slate clean and
rebuild itself and make the same mistakes' (interview).

For Munby, pace was very important. 'There's a complexity to
this play that sometimes means a production can slow down to over-
explain,' he argues. 'I wanted to trust that the audience would get it,
and then to hold them, and pull them forward.' In order to facili-
tate this, he edited the overlaps between scenes so that frequently
the next scene would have begun just before the previous one had
finished – often in Webster, he suggests, 'the last line of a scene would
inform the beginning of the first line of the next scene' (interview).
The result was described in some of the production's reviews as 'a
fierce, hurtling momentum' (*Sunday Express*, 26 October 2008) and
'an almost frenzied energy that becomes, at times, exhausting to
watch' (*Observer*, 12 October 2008). Implicit in this strategy was also a
suggestion that the audience were witnessing a set of interconnected,
overlapping worlds.

This sense of the play as the story not of a single protagonist, but
rather of a whole community of characters, was underscored by
Munby's handling of the play's final moments. As Vittoria, Flamineo

and Zanche lay dead, Giovanni rushed in and shot Lodovico himself. The moment, for Munby, was meant to convey a 'sense of inevitability': 'Although that boy may have tried to resist that kind of life, he's sort of indoctrinated into it, and has no choice. It becomes his tragedy, in a sense. He, now, is in that world' (interview). The conclusion was a tragic climax not merely for Vittoria and Flamineo (and arguably Lodovico), but also for a character usually considered a peripheral one – and, in a sense, for the whole community. It illustrated in tragic terms the same idea that the mopping janitor embodied comically.

Casting

Another major consideration when staging any play is the kind of actor that should be cast in each role. The text of *The White Devil* is often unspecific about the details of its characters' physicalities, but even where it does give hints, directors have sometimes chosen to ignore them for legitimate artistic reasons.

Age is an inescapable issue. In Prowse's production, for example, Josette Simon as Vittoria was significantly younger than both Denis Quilley's avuncular Bracciano and Eleanor Bron's Isabella, suggesting a Vittoria who was using her feminine wiles to entrap a seedy middle-aged playboy. The age difference allowed Giovanni to be played by an actor who was in his 20s – helpful for the play's final scene, perhaps (and for the practicalities of casting), but it made the exchange in which the character plays at being a soldier in II.i difficult to believe; Emrys Jones found the scene 'ridiculous' (*Times Literary Supplement*, 28 June 1991). Camillo, on the other hand, was played by an actor much younger than the middle-aged cuckold implied in the text – a decision which, given the much older Bracciano, David Carnegie describes as 'perverse' (1995: 115).

Like Prowse, Franks also opted for an age gap between his leads, though in his production David Rintoul's Bracciano was still sexually magnetic:

> I very much wanted Vittoria to be much younger than Bracciano, because it just makes sense. You know, he is that classic middle-aged macho shit, who's trading in his once-stylish but now-a-little-bit-in-need-of-botox

wife for a younger model, with scant regard to anybody's feelings but his own.

As Isabella, meanwhile, Jane Bertish played a 'fearsomely fashionable' middle-aged woman in turban and sunglasses who 'looked like something from Italian *Vogue*' (interview).

An often-sensitive subject in casting is race. It has become the norm in recent years to employ 'colour-blind' casting in classical theatre; the director supposedly chooses not to take an actor's ethnicity into account when casting a role. In a play like *The White Devil*, however, in which at least one character is both verbally and physically abused for her racial difference (V.i.86–91, V.i.186–200), the presence or absence of other black faces in the cast will have a direct impact upon the text's meanings. For his production, Prowse cast black actors as the entire Corombona family, making Vittoria, her brothers and her mother (and, of course, Zanche) visibly different from everyone else on stage. Several reviews picked up on the implications here: Benedict Nightingale suggested that it emphasized the family's status as 'outsiders, upstarts, mistrusted for their status as well as their morals' (*The Times*, 19 June 1991), while Michael Coveney saw the casting as 'clarifying the social collisions of the play and suggesting alternative cultural, sexual and moral imperatives' (*Observer*, 23 June 1991). Prowse himself read the Corombonas as an 'aspirant, lower-middle-class family', and explained his reason for the casting choice as being to 'make visible and make comprehensible to a modern audience the almost superstitious fear the ruling class in the play feel when they are invaded' (*Sunday Times*, 2 June 1991). Edwards, meanwhile, took a different approach in her production, casting Vittoria and her family as white, but Bracciano and Giovanni as black. Ray Fearon's young, black Bracciano thus formed a contrast with Stephen Boxer's middle-aged, white Francisco, hinting at a latent reason for the antipathy between the two Dukes and visually separating Bracciano from the play's other powerful characters.

Though none of this chapter's four case studies made a feature of it, a further casting category which might disrupt or elaborate upon some of the play's meanings is gender. Webster must have written the play expecting that all the female roles would be played by male actors, and the performances of 1920 and 1931 by the Cambridge University Marlowe Society are among the only modern productions to have followed this through. A 2006 production in Brighton, on the other hand, took the play in the opposite direction, casting female actors as Vittoria's brothers and changing the gender of the characters to make them her sisters, Flaminea and Marcella. Flaminea's misogynistic diatribes thus became an outpouring of self-loathing, and her sibling rivalry with Vittoria more explicit.

In mainstream professional productions, actors also bring to their roles the baggage of any previous performances in which the audience might have seen them. This can be, and has been, used productively by a director. Franks very deliberately cast two actors who were not from classical theatre backgrounds in his Lyric Hammersmith production: Anthony Valentine, who played Monticelso, was famous for his television work playing thugs and villains, while Dilys Laye, who played Cornelia, was best known for her roles in the *Carry On* films. Monticelso was thus invested with a strong sense of menace, and Cornelia with a comic edge (at Bracciano and Vittoria's wedding, for example, she could be seen getting drunk in the corner, eyeing up the waiters, with her legs wide apart). Both actors, claims Franks, 'brought the real disciplines of proper entertainment, commercial entertainment, to bear on this poetic drama' – Valentine spoke the text 'like the words were just occurring to him', while Laye 'played Cornelia with a lack of sentiment' as a 'tough old bitch from the streets who'd got a bit of cash and was clinging onto it' (interview). Cornelia's subsequent breakdown was all the more powerful because it was so surprising.

Vittoria

As we saw at the beginning of this chapter, a production's decision about the degree to which Vittoria is a 'white devil' will determine to a great extent the tone, impact and politics of the entire play. Geraldine McEwan's 1969 portrayal largely condemned Vittoria, rendering the production cynical and arch; Glenda Jackson's 1976 interpretation did the opposite, making the character's treatment both shocking and unsettling.

All four of this chapter's case studies presented an essentially sympathetic Vittoria who combined elements of both approaches. For Prowse, Vittoria was 'a rogue woman against a turbulent time'

(*Sunday Times*, 2 June 1991). Thus, Josette Simon was both an exotic outsider and a defiant heroine, combining, in Irving Wardle's phrase, 'the imperious courtesan and the heroic rebel' (*Independent*, 23 June 1991). Benedict Nightingale noted that though she could 'shut her gilded eyelids and sensuously purr when male hands are on her', there was also 'something fine, proud, and wonderfully defiant about her' (*The Times*, 19 June 1991). Edwards's production emphasized similar qualities: Michael Billington described Jane Gurnett's Vittoria as 'a strongly sexual figure who can hardly wait to unlace her blood red frock', but noted that she achieved a 'monumental dignity' later in the play (*Guardian*, 29 April 1996). Franks, meanwhile, integrated Zoe Waites's Vittoria into his Fellini-inspired setting by interpreting her as a glamorous and flirtatious celebrity, evoking Anita Ekberg's role in *La Dolce Vita*; Lyn Gardner read Waites's portrayal as 'an intelligent woman trying to be herself in a world that sees her only as a commodity' (*Guardian*, 16 September 2000). Franks describes Vittoria as 'somebody who is fighting with every bit of her being to survive in this world', who is 'unlucky enough to be surrounded by decadent bullies, psychopaths and hypocrites' but actually 'steers quite an impressive path through the vilification that the world hurls at her'; he utterly rejects the idea that she is 'the white devil' (interview). In Munby's production, too, Claire Price's Vittoria was essentially a survivor:

> She finds herself in that situation, fighting for her life and honour, and is damned if she's going to go down without a fight. It actually came from a very positive place, in terms of our exploration of her: what does that woman do in that situation, in that male-constructed trial, to survive? What does she *have* to do? And that, as a starting point, actually became very freeing. One can justify everything that she says, I think, within that idea of survival. (Interview)

A number of reviews commended Price's complex and layered portrayal as, for example, 'a dazzlingly multi-faceted performance' (*Observer*, 12 October 2008), and as 'an unsettling mix of wantonness and blonde, wide-eyed innocence' (*Independent on Sunday*, 19 October 2008).

The text itself gives few clues as to Vittoria's behaviour in her first scene (I.ii) – she speaks very little until her conversation with

Bracciano at ll. 206–69, but she is prominent on stage long before that. What impression of Vittoria do the actor and director wish to convey from her first appearance? In Prowse's production, she entered at the centre of a torch-lit dance and procession, in which she and the other participants were clothed entirely in gold and black: it evoked luxury, ritual and decadence. Edwards's production was more riotous, and Gurnett's Vittoria entered surrounded by drunken revellers, already flirting with Bracciano; by the end of the scene, she and Bracciano had kissed and groped one another, and she had sunk orgasmically to the floor as he presented her with his 'jewel' (I.ii.229 – very clearly a sexual metaphor in this production). The presentation of Camillo also has a major effect on the audience's assessment of Vittoria, and, if he is presented sympathetically, Vittoria's behaviour becomes more callous by implication. If, on the other hand, he is unlikeable, then Vittoria becomes more appealing. Franks interpreted him as 'a bit like the creepy brother in *The Godfather* – the one who is constantly doing things wrong and has no self-respect, and nobody has any respect for him' (interview). One could hardly blame Vittoria for abandoning this husband.

The audience are most explicitly invited to judge Vittoria at her arraignment. Edwards had Gurnett's Vittoria deliver her entire defence downstage to the audience, even though her judges sat behind her. As Kate Aughterson points out, this staging strategy 'deepens our involvement in the debate and outcome of that scene' (2001: 255). Gurnett remained calm and poised, even wryly amused, throughout her trial, and never departed once from her central spot. This meant that Monticelso either stalked the periphery of the space, or invaded Vittoria's in order to attack her: his behaviour thus seemed both predatory and defensive. His speeches were often delivered uncomfortably close to Vittoria's body, and at one point, he spoke his lines from behind her, almost into her neck. This Vittoria was bravely enduring sustained abuse that bordered on the sexual. The bias of the Ambassadors and other members of the court was also made palpable, as they jeered at Vittoria throughout the scene. The audience – the real judges – were thus encouraged to be as dissimilar to their onstage counterparts as possible.

Munby made a similar use of the audience's presence in his interpretation of the trial. The scene opened with a ritualized procession into the space, and Vittoria was brought in, handcuffed. She was led to a spot at one end of the narrow traverse stage, and Monticelso sat at the other: both characters were thus positioned on opposite sides of a debate, flanked on both sides by the audience. He had the freedom to walk around, but Vittoria's movement was restrained by her bonds. Like Edwards, Munby costumed both Vittoria and Monticelso in red for this scene, implying that the sexuality Monticelso condemned was in fact a barely repressed aspect of his own psyche. His speech condemning 'whores' was central to the whole production: 'for me,' explains Munby, 'it places Vittoria very much as victim of this male, staunchly Catholic world'. Interestingly, Vittoria's responses drew rounds of applause from the audience during the production's first preview, but Munby admits that they 'never really got it back after that' (interview).

Franks describes Vittoria's trial as her opportunity 'to answer back to all these men who are making her into what *they* want to see, and then despising the very thing that they've invented' (interview). Making what Rhoda Koenig described as a 'movie-star entrance in a white backless dress' (*Independent*, 19 September 2000), Zoe Waites's Vittoria was confident and defiant in throughout the scene. Jeremy Kingston's review illustrates one of the ways in which this staging made specific modern parallels: 'She mocks the scorn of the Cardinal, smiling mischievously so that she briefly resembles pictures of the young Mae West – herself once a victim of the state's dislike of boldly sexual women' (*The Times*, 15 September 2000). Franks asked Anthony Valentine to play Monticelso's 'whore' speech as 'a piece of absolutely brilliant courtroom rhetoric' which then ran rapidly out of control. Waites's Vittoria looked on in incredulity that it was being believed: 'it was as though society was taking its mask off,' says Franks, 'and revealing just how furious and angry and hot it is underneath' (interview).

Flamineo

Unlike Vittoria, whose guilt (or otherwise) lies only in the nuances of performance, Flamineo is without question both a murderer and a fraud. He is also shamelessly self-centred and grossly misogynistic. Despite all this, he is often the most magnetic character. He has the most lines, and by far the highest number of asides to the audience;

he is funny, witty and defiant, and is in many ways just as much of a protagonist as his sister (like Vittoria, he is a character whose struggle we follow from beginning to end).

In Munby's production, the character was half of an equal and opposite yin-yang pairing with Vittoria: the nervy, dark-haired Aidan McArdle both contrasted and complemented the elegant, fair-haired Price. 'On one level, he's in love with her,' says Munby. 'But also he loves the idea of her' (interview). Thus, as he watched his sister caressing Bracciano in I.ii, McArdle's Flamineo hugged himself with longing. The moment was echoed later in the play, when, at the house of convertites, Flamineo once again derived a vicarious pleasure from reuniting Vittoria and Bracciano (his status as an onlooker, perhaps, being foregrounded by the traverse staging). Finally, as he put Vittoria's loyalty to him to the test in V.vi, he began fulfil a fantasy about *becoming* her, putting on her jewellery, wearing one of a pair of her earrings while she wore the other, and applying her make-up to both of their faces.

McArdle's was a brittle Flamineo. He was seen at various points snorting cocaine and popping pills, and his body language and make-up (blue eye-shadow and black nail varnish) suggested a highly defensive character whose sexuality was ambiguous. When he explained to his mother that 'conspiring with a beard / Made me a graduate' (I.ii.324–5) – a line which suggests that he connived with an official in order to gain his degree – he mimed an act of fellatio. He had allowed himself to be exploited by the powerful in his pursuit of social advancement, and he was bitterly angry about his treatment. 'We tried to embrace the full ugliness, or unpleasantness,' says Munby: 'what he's had to do to survive, to succeed – and what that's made him, and how that's damaged him' (interview).

Franks uses the same term to describe Sebastian Harcombe's performance as Flamineo in the Lyric production: 'The thing I was interested about in him is how desperately damaged he is: flailing around and sometimes achieving a kind of temporary strength just through the recklessness of what he's prepared to do.' Harcombe, says Franks, 'had a fantastic vulnerability, as well as a kind of unpredictable psychotic quality' (interview). Like McArdle, Harcombe played Flamineo as taking an unhealthy interest in his sister's sexuality: he continually solicited physical contact with her, watched her in the bathroom in a highly charged way, and lit up 'a post-coital cigarette for himself' as she made love to Bracciano (*Evening Standard*, 14 September 2000). For Franks, Flamineo got 'a kind of awful kick' out of prostituting his own sister:

> He's found a sort of terrible pleasure out of the worst things that could possibly happen in life. It's as though he's tempting God, to see if God exists, by doing the worst things he can do, to see if he's going to get punished. And of course he is. He is haunted. If you're a cold-hearted villain without a conscience, you don't get haunted. (Interview)

As Charles Isherwood's review observed, Harcombe's Flamineo, dredging up 'a few wisps of conscience in the final acts', became 'the disturbingly charismatic eye of this storm of violence' (*Variety*, 23 September 2000).

Other Flamineos have been more unambiguously evil. Prowse's Flamineo, Dhobi Oparei, was one who revelled in his own villainy; John Peter could detect 'no hint of anything so complicated as a troubled conscience' (*Sunday Times*, 23 June 1991), while Michael Coveney saw him as 'embodying an instinct for evil different from that of the stock stage Machiavel' (*Observer*, 23 June 1991). Michael Billington noted Oparei's 'gaunt, sinister presence' and praised his 'nice touch for comedy in the scene where he dissembles death from a bullet', but felt that his real death-speech was somewhat thrown away (*Guardian*, 20 June 1991).

Edwards's Flamineo, played by Richard McCabe, was more complex. McCabe forged a close relationship with the audience over the course of the performance, increasing Flamineo's number of soliloquies even further by turning speeches such as those in III. iii ('Religion; O, how it is commeddled with policy'; ll. 38–40) and IV.ii ('Stay, my lord; I'll tell you a tale'; ll. 224–37) into moments of direct audience address. Robert Hanks described it as 'a superbly louche, funny performance, which finds a degree of cynical humour in the role that reminds you we're not so far removed in time from Restoration comedy' (*Independent*, 29 April 1996). But underlying McCabe's comedy was a sharp sense of Flamineo as a cynical outsider: a rather effete, impotent figure in comparison to the macho Bracciano or Marcello, and one whose facial expression was frequently marked by what Jeremy Kingston described as a 'look of hunger' (*The Times*, 9 January 1997). McCabe's Flamineo was every inch the Jacobean malcontent.

Like other Flamineos, McCabe's had an incestuous obsession with his sister. What set this performance apart, though, was that his feelings were in some way reciprocated by Jane Gurnett's Vittoria. He groped her genitals quite overtly over I.ii.155–61 (as he ostensibly persuaded her to make love to Bracciano), and Vittoria was shown to enjoy it. Flamineo's subsequent observation to Camillo that 'I find her coming' (I.ii.65) was so clearly a *double entendre* that it got one of the biggest laughs of the scene. Elizabeth Schafer notes that Gurnett 'had her breasts manhandled as much by Flamineo as by Bracciano', and that his threats to Vittoria at the end of the play 'included lasciviously licking as much of her skin as possible' (1997: 117). Aughterson criticizes this interpretation, arguing that 'by reducing that relationship solely to sexuality, Edwards denied some of the play's other themes': 'the question of masculine political patronage; the workings of masculine honour; the way in which other women are victimized by the play's misogyny; and the presence of such misogyny in the words and action of the play' (2001: 256). But the production's investment in Flamineo's relationship with Vittoria had a moving pay-off in the final scene, as the mortally wounded Flamineo crawled towards his sister as she died. Cradling her as the lights narrowed to a single spotlight, he was, as John Peter's review put it, 'finally blasted by a sense of remorse he does not quite understand' (*Sunday Times*, 5 May 1996).

Staging the supernatural

A potential problem for modern directors of *The White Devil* is how to handle the supernatural elements: specifically, the Conjuror's summoning of the visions of the murders, and the appearances of the ghosts of Isabella and Bracciano. To a Jacobean audience, these features of the play would have been conventional and entirely in keeping with their expectations of a revenge tragedy; moreover, the audience was probably composed largely of people who actively believed in the reality of a supernatural world. To a modern audience accustomed to naturalism, however, the same scenes can be highly problematic.

One solution is to create a convention which signals to the audience that the episode is not to be read naturalistically. In Dunlop's 1969 production, for example, the dumb-shows were staged in slow motion, while Munby's 2008 production used stylized movement to signify the other-worldly nature of the supernatural scenes. Munby staged the dumb-shows as a drug-induced hallucination, in which Bracciano was strapped to a chair and injected; the doors at the opposite end of the stage then burst open, as a flurry of violent movement headed towards him. Munby worked with the production's movement director, Georgina Lamb, to create a physical motif for Isabella's murder which then resurfaced later in the production: as Vittoria and Bracciano celebrated their wedding with a dance, Isabella's ghost returned to the stage and wound her way through them, physically re-enacting her jerky, horrific death. She was quite literally haunting the couple: as Lyn Gardner's review observed, 'there will always be three in this marriage: the guilty lovers and the murdered wife' (*Guardian*, 11 October 2008).

Prowse's production employed a number of highly theatrical effects to convince its audience of the reality of the supernatural elements. Sound effects such as howling dogs, tolling bells and thunderclaps were used to invoke a sense of the 'witching time of night'. The dumb-shows were underscored by the chimes of midnight, as Zanche (taking the role of the Conjuror in this production) used a kind of voodoo spell to summon up the visions. As she did so, the large number of candles which surrounded the stage all spontaneously ignited. This chapter has already mentioned the near-constant presence of onstage ghosts in this production (see above). As Bracciano's ghost entered in V.iv, he blew out the candles before Flamineo turned and saw him.

Other productions – such as those by Franks and Edwards – have adopted almost the opposite strategy, underplaying the supernatural aspects in order to reinvent them as psychological ones. Franks's modern-dress production replaced the dumb-shows with film projections (as did both the Guthrie Theatre production of 1977 and the BBC Radio 3 adaptation of 2010, in which listeners could hear the whirring of a cine-projector). The assassins had provided Bracciano with the film reels as evidence of their completion of their tasks, and as he viewed them, he sat back on cushions as if he were watching a piece of entertainment. Camillo was shown being murdered in a sleazy gymnasium, with Flamineo constantly checking the camera and grinning. For Isabella's death, meanwhile, the camera was concealed behind a dressing-room mirror so that she was, as Franks explains, 'in huge close-up, looking into her mirror – taking her make-up off, hair up in a band – just staring at her unhappy, ageing face that her husband no longer loved' (interview). The poisoned portrait was a small photograph of Bracciano that she carried around in a travelling case, and this was sprayed by her murderer with a small aerosol. In his evident enjoyment of not only her murder but also her misery, Bracciano appeared more than usually callous here.

Later in Franks's production, Bracciano's ghost came crashing out of the rubbish heap, covered in dust, exhaling a great mouthful of smoke. But for Franks, the appearance of this ghost was not a real supernatural visiting, but rather a manifestation of Flamineo's guilty conscience (it appears, after all, just moments after Flamineo's recognition of 'the maze of conscience in my breast' at V.iv.122). Both ghosts, argues Franks, are embodiments of suppressed elements of the characters' psychologies:

> If you think 'The world's completely amoral, I can do whatever I like', then you are in massive denial – and it'll fester, and eventually it'll burst, like an abscess. That's what the ghosts were. The ghosts were burstings forth of things denied. (Interview)

This idea was illustrated even more clearly in Edwards's RSC production, in which neither of the ghosts appeared to the audience. Francisco's summoning of Isabella's ghost in IV.i was signified only by a lighting change: Francisco was suddenly lit from beneath, casting a huge shadow backwards onto the wall as he pointed wildly into the auditorium. Flamineo's response to the (non-)appearance of Bracciano's ghost in V.iv was staged in exactly the same way. By emphasizing the living character's reaction rather than the presence of the ghost, Edwards made both scenes almost entirely about psychology.

A key tool in staging the play's paranormal elements is music. It was certainly the only concession in Edwards's production to any sense of the reality of the supernatural. As Isabella described Bracciano's divorce as a 'cursèd vow' (II.i.218), her words were underscored with a haunting drone, suggesting a particular significance to her speech. This drone returned when Vittoria cursed Monticelso at the conclusion of her trial (III.ii.279–83), and then again later at Flamineo's conclusion that 'Knaves do grow great by being great men's apes' (IV.ii.249) – the implication being that all of these utterances, concerned as they were with predictions of the future, were loaded and fateful remarks. Music played a similarly important role in Munby's production, as he explains: 'Dominic Haslam, my composer, works thematically, so we created a theme for Flamineo, for example, and a theme for Isabella. The Isabella theme actually became a recurrent and haunting idea, that came back to torment Bracciano' (interview). Thus, as Isabella's ghost returned to haunt the marriage procession, her theme tore through the wedding music. The later appearance of Bracciano's own ghost was likewise accompanied by music.

Gender and violence

In an interview with the *Independent* shortly before her production of *The White Devil* opened, Edwards drew attention to the problematic gender politics of the play:

> Webster says some extraordinary things about women – the misogyny is appalling – there's a real fear of their sexuality and what they unleash in the world. Vittoria must be crushed – she has brought anarchy about because she is having an affair. (*Independent*, 24 April 1996)

Edwards's observations about the ways in which the male characters view Vittoria are undoubtedly accurate – but are their opinions endorsed by the play itself? Arguably, the injustice of Vittoria's treatment encourages the audience to recognize the inequalities of patriarchy. On the other hand, Vittoria appears to be punished for her aberrance in the final scene.

The text is neither misogynist nor anti-sexist until its meanings are realized in performance. Charles Spencer identified the 'undoubted feminist slant' of Edwards's production, noting that 'all the women are depicted as victims of male barbarity' (*Daily Telegraph*,

29 April 1996). Certainly Ray Fearon's Bracciano was overbearing and threatening to all the women he encountered; he drew his sword upon Isabella during their private confrontation in II.i, prompting her to burst into tears and sink to the floor, where he subjected her to a further barrage of verbal abuse. He cursed their 'issue' (l. 191) by shouting the line into her face, and as she raised her hand to strike him in retaliation, he grabbed it and kissed it with vicious force. Isabella's subsequent public divorce from Bracciano was performed by Teresa Banham from centre stage, as the men playing Francisco, Monticelso and Bracciano surrounded her in a visual emblem of patriarchal oppression. A further metaphor for her subjugation was added when, as she removed her wedding ring at line 254, she had difficulty wrenching it from her finger.

A sense of the injustice of patriarchy was also in evidence in Prowse's production. At the end of II.ii, Bracciano escaped arrest, but Zanche (as the reluctant Conjuror) was apprehended and both Vittoria and her mother were immediately pulled in on chairs for the subsequent trial scene. Cornelia and Zanche remained behind Vittoria, conspicuously shackled, for the duration of the scene. Later in the production, the hypocrisy and cruelty of this male-dominated world became even clearer. The Matron of the house of convertites was clearly a brothel madam as well as a nun. As she genuflected to greet a couple of male visitors, one of them lifted her skirt to reveal a scarlet petticoat, while a third emerged from a hidden room to leave his payment on her table. A line of six young women, all of them in white dresses, were then paraded before the two new customers. Each of the women wore a brutal metal contraption called a scold's bridle – a kind of cage for the head, with a flat piece of iron designed to push into the mouth and hold the tongue down – which was used during the Jacobean period to punish 'unruly' women.

Both Franks and Munby emphasized Vittoria's literal and meta-phorical imprisonment in the scene at the house of convertites. Franks's Matron was vicious, mercenary and unwelcoming, and Zoe Waites's Vittoria emerged in a shapeless black dress with her hair in a bandage (a sharp change from her glamorous appearance at the trial). At the beginning of Munby's version of the scene, fretwork appeared through one of the doors at the end of the space, creating a sudden sense of entrapment. When Vittoria was led out, she was in a prison dress and barefoot, denuded of the jewels and make-up in which the audience had previously seen her. 'It marked her degradation and humiliation,' says Munby; 'she was literally stripped of her wealth and dignity' (interview).

Edwards's production provided an even bleaker image, using the trapdoor in the middle of the space to suggest connotations of hell. Shrouded in dry ice, the Matron and Flamineo emerged from the depths of the stage at the beginning of the scene, with the Matron descending again to fetch Vittoria. Vittoria then entered in silence, wearing a dirty white undergarment, and kneeled to Bracciano. As he accused her of infidelity, the image of Bracciano shouting at a kneeling woman became a visual reminder of his earlier scene with Isabella – though this was suddenly reversed when he, too, knelt as he invoked his 'duchess' (IV.ii.99) and Vittoria stood for her verbal counter-attack on him. The scene ended with a disturbing combination of violence and sexuality, as Flamineo grabbed his sister from behind and advised Bracciano to 'stop her mouth' (l. 194) with a kiss. This unsolicited invasion of Vittoria's body turned quickly into a passionate mutual embrace.

Zanche is subjugated on three counts: not only as a woman, but also as a servant and as a racial outsider. Edwards emphasized the brutality of her treatment in V.i, as Marcello threw her to the floor and Cornelia slapped her around the face, both completely unprovoked; Marcello then kicked her twice, with evident relish, as she lay on the ground. Like Gurnett's Vittoria, Martina Laird's Zanche was condemned for her sensuality. Stephen Boxer's cold and Machiavellian Francisco had no compunctions about exploiting her attraction to him, allowing her to spread her legs around him while she gave him valuable information, but throwing her off as soon as soon as she had fulfilled her purpose (V.iii.244–63). Munby discusses the same moment in his production as being a further example of a woman falling victim 'to the whims of these rather awful, self-serving men' – but unlike Edwards's production, the liaison between Karen Bryson's Zanche and Louis Hilyer's Francisco 'explored a real desire'. It was, says Munby, 'erotically charged, the encounter between those two' (interview). The idea that Francisco could gain sexual pleasure from his liaison with Zanche, while ultimately condemning her, is perhaps illustrative of patriarchy's hypocritical attitudes towards female sexuality.

The violent victimization of 'unruly' women reaches its climax in the final scene. The prompt book in the National Theatre Archive reveals the extent of the cruelty in Prowse's production, and its stage directions for the actor playing Antonelli describe Zanche's murder in detail:

> Grab [Zanche's] hair in left hand, pull her to feet. Slash her across stomach with sword in right hand. Momentum carries her to D/S point of rostra where she sits. He presents sword to her. She grabs blade, and he pulls sword through her hands. She puts her hands over her face. He slashes her stomach. [...] He picks her head up and cuts her along back of neck. She dies.

Vittoria's death carried further connotations of sexualized brutality. Lodovico stripped to a loincloth for the murder, crying out as he repeatedly stabbed her, accompanying his knife-thrusts into her body, as Nick Curtis put it, 'with carnal thrusts of his pelvis', while Vittoria's own death cries built 'in an orgasmic spiral' (*Plays and Players*, August 1991). Josette Simon delivered the line "'Twas a manly blow" (V.vi.232) with a pointed sarcasm, and as Paul Taylor's review explains, 'the cool pretence that she is congratulating him on his sexual prowess ironically deflates his vengeful achievement' (*Independent*, 20 June 1991).

Prowse's production was by no means unusual in its sexualization of Vittoria's death. Both of the Old Vic productions discussed at the start of this chapter (Dunlop 1969 and Lindsay-Hogg 1976) concluded with Lodovico stabbing Vittoria in her genitals, though Cave notes that whereas the earlier version was portrayed as 'a perverse sexual gratification', the later one was 'sadistic male revenge against a woman who dared to attempt to determine her own destiny' (1988: 112). Franks's production ended in a similar manner, as Vittoria and Zanche, clad only in their underwear, were interrupted in a hotel bedroom as they desperately attempted to pack their suitcases and flee. Lodovico burst in and stabbed Vittoria in her groin, before throwing her body down on the floor. Her blood flooded the stage and dripped down off it into the surrounding guttering; as Franks puts it, 'the world was awash with the consequence of violence' (interview).

The sense of Lodovico's sexual gratification upon his murder of Vittoria was even more pronounced in Munby's production, as the killer went as far as taking photographs of the two dead women moments after their murders. Lodovico and Antonelli had killed Vittoria and Zanche simultaneously, as both women – each wearing white – were put back-to-back and stabbed at crotch-height. Munby describes what he calls the murderers' 'perverse sexuality':

> They degraded them, and also reminded them of why they were being murdered in the very way that they stabbed them. But there was a really important moment for me when the two women grabbed the hands of their murderers and pushed the knives deeper, to somehow take control of that act.

Munby explains this as the final manifestation of a 'running theme' of the production: Vittoria, 'even in the last throes of her life, was somehow trying to make her own stand and having some control over her destiny' (interview).

The problematic gender politics of a play in which the female characters are perpetually victimized, often in a highly sexualized manner, hardly need stressing. In staging these scenes, a production often treads a fine line between simply enacting misogyny and exposing it. It is important for production teams to consider whether Vittoria, Zanche and Isabella (and perhaps also Cornelia) are active or reactive in their struggles against patriarchal forces, and what implications these staging choices might have upon the gender politics of the production itself.

As these case studies show, *The White Devil* offers a great deal to the modern theatre company. It plays as a terrific political and psychological thriller, as a pitch-black comedy, and as an unsettling and profoundly moving exploration of sexuality, desire and cruelty. The density of its language and the intensity of its verbal imagery is consistently striking. Its scenes of supernatural apparitions and murders indulge any taste for the macabre, and its enormous variation in style positively encourages experimentation with non-naturalistic forms of acting. Webster's sharp, even radical analysis of power and ideology remains thought-provoking and topical today, while the play's arguable status as a proto-feminist text also offers an area of exploration which has perhaps been under-emphasized in the modern theatre. The play is a gift for a designer: its imagery invites a robust use of visual metaphor and of colour (as the title itself seems to demand). At the same time, it depicts central characters who are psychologically complex and morally ambiguous. The audience are not told where their sympathies should lie, and are constantly invited to re-assess their prejudices.

5   Critical Assessments

The White Devil has inspired a wide range of commentary over the centuries since it was written. This chapter provides a highly selective overview of some of the key critical assessments. It is by no means exhaustive, and many excellent studies have been omitted. It is designed, however, to be representative of some of the key trends in Websterian criticism over history.

Early criticism

In the decades immediately following the publication of The White Devil, there was no formal literary criticism, so one finds only scattered comments about the play's quality. Clergyman Abraham Wright, for example, described it as 'an indifferent play to read' in his commonplace book (c. 1640), and complained that its lines were 'too much rhyming', though he did commend its final act. Samuel Sheppard's poem 'On Mr. Webster's Most Excellent Tragedy, Called the White Devil' (1651) is more complimentary, praising Webster's characterization of Bracciano, Flamineo, Vittoria, Lodovico and Francisco in particular:

> We will no more admire Euripides,
> Nor praise the tragic strains of Sophocles;
> For why? Thou in this tragedy has framed
> All real worth that can in them be named.
> How lively are thy persons fitted, and
> How pretty are thy lines! Thy verses stand
> Like unto precious jewels set in gold
> And grace thy fluent prose. I once was told,
> By one well skilled in Arts, he thought thy play
> Was only worthy fame to bear away

From all before it. Brachiano's ill,
Murdering his Duchess, hath by thy rare skill
Made him renowned; Flamineo such another,
The Devil's darling, murderer of his brother.
His part, most strange, given him to act by thee
Doth gain him credit and not calumny.
Vittoria Corombona, that famed whore;
Desperate Lodovico weltering in his gore;
Subtle Francisco; all of them shall be
Gazed at as comets by posterity.
And thou meantime, with never-withering bays,
Shall crowned be by all that read thy lays.

This poem is perhaps not particularly useful as an analysis of the play, but it does tell us a great deal about the way in which at least one early reader (who might also once have been an audience member) understood it. Sheppard evidently saw Webster's *characters* as the play's chief area of interest, and the ways in which he interprets them are telling: while he seems to recognize that Flamineo is a morally ambiguous character, he sees Vittoria simply as a 'whore'. For Sheppard, Francisco's defining characteristic is his 'subtlety', or deviousness, while the description of Lodovico as 'weltering in his gore' evokes an overblown and bloody staging of the final scene. Sheppard's comments might thus be useful background reading for anyone wishing to stage the play today.

Romantic criticism

It was not until the nineteenth century that Webster's play inspired sustained literary debate. The character of Vittoria was a source of fascination for some of the most famous critics of the Romantic period. In 1808, Charles Lamb praised her 'innocence-resembling boldness' in the trial scene, suggesting that the audience are

> ready to expect, when she has done her pleadings, that her very judges, her accusers, the grave ambassadors who sit as spectators, and all the court, will rise and make proffer to defend her in spite of the utmost conviction of her guilt. (1808: 215)

William Hazlitt was in agreement, describing the character as 'fair as the leprosy, dazzling as the lightning', and he also singled out the trial scene for praise:

> Nothing can be imagined finer than the whole conduct and conception of this scene, than her scorn of her accusers and of herself. The sincerity of her sense of guilt triumphs over the hypocrisy of their affected and official contempt for it. (1820: 97)

In a similar vein, Alexander Dyce's introduction to *The Works of John Webster* (1830) also focused on the lifelike complexity of the guilty Vittoria during this scene. What seems to have captivated these critics is Webster's presentation of a character who challenges comfortable moral judgements in a potentially unsettling way.

But this moral ambiguity was not universally admired. In an essay for *Blackwood's Edinburgh Magazine* in 1818, 'H. M.' complained of 'some scenes that altogether revolt and disgust'. His chief objection was that 'unprincipled characters occupy too much of our attention throughout the action of the play':

> There is but little imagination breathed over the passions of the prime agents, who exhibit themselves in the bare deformity of evil, – and scene follows scene of shameless profligacy, unredeemed either by great intellectual energy, or occasional burstings of moral sensibilities. (1818: 34)

Though he noted that Vittoria was 'sketched with great spirit and freedom', he felt that she was 'not fit to be the chief personage of tragedy, which ought ever to deal only with great passions, and with great events'. He admitted, however, to a 'sort of fascination' in the character, and to 'something like admiration towards her' in her death scene (1818: 35).

Victorian criticism

Hazlitt described Webster's tragedies as coming 'the nearest to Shakespeare of any thing we have upon record'; their only drawback, he observed, was that 'they are too like Shakespeare, and often direct imitations of him, both in general conception and individual expression (1820: 95). In assessing Webster's worth by comparing him with Shakespeare, Hazlitt was anticipating an obsession which would permeate Websterian criticism for over a century. In 1886, for example, the poet and critic A.C. Swinburne declared Webster 'the right arm' of Shakespeare, noting that though Webster could not match Shakespeare's 'reach of vision',

> the force of hand, the fire of heart, the fervour of pity, the sympathy of passion, not poetic or theatric merely, but actual and immediate, are qualities in which the lesser poet is not less certainly or less unmistakably pre-eminent than the greater.

There was, he concluded, 'no third to be set beside them' (1886: 16).

Others were less flattering. The poet William Watson condemned such comparisons, suggesting that readers should reconsider 'the propriety of the criticism which brackets the name of John Webster with the greatest name in literature' (1893: 11). Webster, argued Watson, lacked Shakespeare's moral superiority, wallowing instead in 'cynicism, disgust, and despair' (1893: 13):

> Life seems a chance medley, a rendezvous of bewildered phantoms; virtue in this disordered world is merely wasted, honour bears not issue, nobleness dies unto itself.... In reading him we lose for the time all sensation of an ordered governance of things. (1893: 17–18),

The concern that Webster indulged in the depiction of horrors at the expense of an overarching moral vision led George Bernard Shaw to dub him, famously, the 'Tussaud laureate' (1932, III: 317).

The debate was a heated one. Responding to Swinburne's defence of the playwright as a 'high-souled and gentle-hearted poet' (1886: 46), the critic William Archer censured Webster for 'drenching the stage with blood' and 'searching out every possible circumstance of horror ... with no conceivable purpose except just to make our flesh creep':

> High-souled and gentle-hearted he may possibly have been, for these qualities are not incompatible with the vilest perversions of the aesthetic sense. But to argue that Webster's aesthetic sense was refined and unperverted is simply to maintain that black is white and blood is rose-water. (1893: 45–6)

Archer concluded that Webster should not be considered a 'great dramatist' at all; rather, he argued, the playwright was 'a great poet who wrote haphazard dramatic or melodramatic romances for an eagerly receptive but semi-barbarous public' (1893: 48). Archer seems not to have taken into account Webster's own preface to *The White Devil*, though, in coming to this conclusion: Webster's audience were in fact far from 'eagerly receptive', and Webster declared no intention of pandering to them.

Towards the end of the nineteenth century, a great deal of attention shifted onto the play's treatment of character. Many contemporary dramatists were moving towards a greater realism, and the prevalence of realist novels earlier in the century had led to plays being read almost as if they were novels. This emphasis was expressed most famously in A. C. Bradley's hugely influential book *Shakespearean Tragedy*, in which he argued that 'action is essentially the expression of character'; 'the centre of the tragedy,' he suggested, 'may be said with equal truth to lie in action issuing from character, or in character issuing in action' (1904: 19, 12).

For Swinburne, both *The White Devil* and *The Duchess of Malfi* were to be celebrated for their 'tone of convincing reality' (1886: 16); similarly, the actor and director William Poel rebuked Archer's suggestion that Webster was a greater poet than he was a playwright, on the grounds that 'Webster's most celebrated passages are not great simply because they are pre-eminent in beauty of idea and felicity of expression, but because they carry with them dramatic force by being appropriate to character and situation' (1893: 22). Other writers were less convinced by Webster's characterization. The author Charles Kingsley wrote that he admired the 'rugged power' of Webster's writing, but that he could find in *The White Devil* 'no trace (nor is there, again, in the *Duchess of Malfi*) of that development of human souls for good or evil which is Shakspeare's especial power' (1856: 48). Rather, he argued, Webster's characters 'come on the stage ready-made, full grown, and stereotyped; and therefore, in general, they are not characters at all, but mere passions or humours in human form' (1856: 49). In the trial scene, for example, he suggested that the audience were not given 'an insight into Vittoria's essential heart and brain, but a general acquaintance with the conduct of all bold bad women when brought to bay' (1856: 50).

New Criticism

Over the first few decades of the twentieth century, literary criticism moved away from its focus on character. L. C. Knights published a now well-known essay in 1933 entitled 'How Many Children Had Lady Macbeth?', in which he critiqued the prevailing 'presupposition' that the study of drama was about the analysis of character. Character, he pointed out, was merely an illusion 'brought into being by written or spoken words'; the job of the critic, therefore, was to begin 'with the words of which a play is composed' (1933: 18). Knights was part of a movement in literary criticism which became known as 'New Criticism', and for these critics, the 'words on the page' were paramount. Through this conceptual lens, plays were seen as 'dramatic poems', and the critic's task was to analyse their complex conceptual unity (Knights 1933: 20).

Perhaps it should be no surprise, then, that Webster tended to be rather harshly assessed by such critics, who favoured patterns and unity over eclecticism and dislocation. Webster's plays were, as Barrett Wendell noted, characterized by a lack of unity, 'full of isolated situations, and phrases, and touches of character which seem almost ultimate in their combined character and truth to life':

> What makes the total effect of them bewildering is that he could never quite fuse them into organic unity. His fragments of tragedy are like some unfinished mosaic needing a flash of electric fire to melt their outlines into the intelligible unity of painting. (1904: 88)

F. L. Lucas would articulate similar concerns in 1927, arguing in his introduction to *The Complete Works of John Webster* that 'Webster cannot give his plays a close-knit logical unity; he is often childishly irrelevant; and his characters are sometimes wildly inconsistent from scene to scene' (1927: 21). M. C. Bradbrook, meanwhile, could identify in Webster's tragedies 'no pattern of characters, nor...any structure of themes' (1935: 186). The plays' unity, she felt, was '*only* a unity of tone and temper' and 'precarious and unstable' as a result (1935: 212).

One of Webster's great champions during this period was the poet and critic T. S. Eliot. What helped to 'unify the Webster pattern' for Eliot was the author's 'pity for all of his characters': 'an attitude towards good and bad alike' (1932: 127). Eliot's writings on Webster would become some of the most oft-repeated – the first lines of his poem 'Whispers of Immortality' (1920) in particular (as mentioned in Chapter 4). Eliot would go on to quote twice from *The White Devil* in *The Waste Land* (1922), an intertextual patchwork of 'borrowings' which must have been composed in a manner not dissimilar to Webster's own working method (see 'Webster's sources', Chapter 3). Eliot's borrowings suggest that he, like Webster, was also 'much possessed by death': the passages that he lifts are Cornelia's dirge about a corpse being dug up (V.iv.104–5 in Webster, ll. 74–5 in Eliot) and Flamineo's image of cobwebs being spun over epitaphs (V.vi.156–8 in Webster, ll. 405–7 in Eliot).

Like the Victorians, many early twentieth-century critics were highly preoccupied by the issue of Webster's moral vision. For some, morality in Webster's plays was clear-cut. David Cecil argued in *Poets and Story-Tellers* that Webster's characters divide into 'the good' and 'the bad', and that the bad can be split into two sub-divisions. Of the 'bad' characters in *The White Devil*, Cecil suggests that Vittoria and Bracciano are of the first type, 'creatures of some ruling passion', while characters like Flamineo are of the second, 'actuated less by passion, than by cynicism'. He lists Isabella, Marcello and Cornelia as unambiguously 'good' characters (1949: 29–30). James Smith understood Cornelia as the play's moral touchstone; she is, he argued, a character from whom 'we can take our moral bearings when, amid the amount and variety of vice, they are in danger of being obscured' (1939: 278). The reader might be inclined to question, however, whether the moral line separating, say, Vittoria from her mother, is really so distinct (see, for example, the commentary to V.i.186–213).

For others, Webster presented a bewilderingly amoral universe. Eliot described Webster as 'a very great literary and dramatic genius directed toward chaos' (1950: 98), and for many critics, this was a specifically 'moral chaos' (Bogard 1955: 118). Ian Jack argued as much in an essay in *Scrutiny*, suggesting that this element of Webster's style was highly problematic:

> Great tragedy can be written only by a man who has achieved – at least for the period of composition – a profound and balanced insight into life. Webster – his plays are our evidence – did not achieve such an insight. The imagery, verse-texture, themes, and 'philosophy' of his plays all point to a fundamental flaw, which is ultimately a moral flaw. (1949: 38)

For Irving Ribner, Webster's plays were 'an agonized search for moral order in the uncertain and chaotic world of Jacobean scepticism', and in *The White Devil* the playwright had created 'a poetic impression of this world', though he had found 'no pattern to relate good and evil and provide a basis for morality' (1962: 97). Many critics of this period found in Flamineo's dying line 'O, I am in a mist' (V.vi.260) an apt metaphor for the play's ethical uncertainty.

Vittoria's moral status remained as fiercely debated as it had been in the criticism of previous ages. For Jack, once again, this was a sign of Webster's moral instability: 'Vittoria is dishonourable,' claimed Jack, but 'Webster simply makes her behave as if she were honourable': 'Webster, having no profound hold on any system of moral values, found it easy to write for Vittoria dissembling verse which in its righteous simplicity seems to proclaim her honesty in the face of her accusers' (1949: 41–2). Bradbrook agreed with Jack that Vittoria was 'guilty', but she argued that 'there is a strong undercurrent of suggestion in the opposite direction' (1935: 187). In 1972, however, Ralph Berry objected that Bradbrook had come to the wrong conclusion: 'Vittoria is innocent,' he claimed, 'but the imagery damns her as guilty' (1972: 52). Indeed, as Berry points out, Vittoria is not guilty of murder, cannot be proved unambiguously to have incited the murders ('the actress can play it either way', he notes), and is never shown to have committed adultery either (1972: 53).

For some critics, the play's moral ambivalence was its greatest strength. In his book *The Tragic Satire of John Webster*, Travis Bogard suggested that in fusing the opposite forms of tragedy and satire, Webster had consistently exhibited the play's action 'from two points of view'. As a result, he argued,

> Webster could show not only how splendid individuals can be, ideally, but also to what they are brought in actuality. Man, the satire shows, even at his most wilful, is not the master of his fate. His power is restricted by death; disease limits his body; the wrath of man and the laws of society check his course. (1955: 100)

'Ultimately,' he concluded, 'no clarifying philosophy is possible, for man's mortality renders meaningless the very terms on which such a philosophy must be based' (1955: 118). As Roma Gill went on to argue in 1966:

Bored with an impotent and impoverished husband, eager for social status, wanting to be amoral yet admitting moral conventions, recognizing her own faults and blaming them on others, yet capable of courageous love – Vittoria will not fit into any neat dramatic classification. She is too close to life for comfort. (1966: 51)

'The absence of any character whose opinion we can rely on,' she continued, 'is part of Webster's policy of ambiguity in this play' (1966: 55).

Webster in historical context

Since the 1960s, literary criticism has become increasingly concerned with understanding Webster not as a transcendent literary genius, nor as a moral commentator, but as a writer who reflected, and in a small way shaped, the history of the period in which he lived.

Two exemplary historical studies focus on Webster's sources: R. W. Dent's *John Webster's Borrowing* (1960) and Gunnar Boklund's *The Sources of 'The White Devil'* (1966). Dent's book comprises an introduction to the subject and a detailed commentary on each of Webster's solo-authored plays, and focuses on the 'sources for the detail in Webster's plays – for dialogue, for subordinate episodes, for what Jonson called the "furniture"' (1960: 5). Since Dent's study is explicitly *not* concerned with 'historical or semi-historical sources for the basic plots of the two tragedies' (1960: 4), it is complemented perfectly by Boklund's, which is (for *The White Devil*, at least). Boklund gives the historical facts (as far as they are known) about the life and death of the real Vittoria Accoramboni before surveying in minute detail the numerous documents referring to her. For the student of the sources of Webster's play, these two studies have yet to be bettered.

M. C. Bradbrook's *John Webster, Citizen and Dramatist* (1980) focuses on Webster's life in London, functioning not only as a biography of the playwright but also as a portrait of the city in which he lived and worked. Part One is 'The London of John Webster', detailing not only Webster's life but also those of Richard Mulcaster of the Merchant Taylors' School, the poet John Davies, Webster's neighbour Penelope Rich and Antonio Pérez, the Spanish spy: 'I have adopted the display method of taking four representative figures,' explains Bradbrook, 'and telling their stories at some length' (1980: 2). Part Two, 'John Webster the Dramatist', 'records the progress of Webster's intermittent dramatic career' (1980: 4). Bradbrook's chapter on *The White Devil* is thus both a close reading of the play, and a historical and cultural contextualization of it.

One of the most important books in steering the study of Webster towards greater historical contextualization was J. W. Lever's *The Tragedy of State*, first published in 1971. At a time when academics (and students especially) were becoming increasingly politicized, Lever's book was an intervention into what he saw as the rather reactionary world of literary study. Lever critiqued, for example, the Ian Jack article cited above, in which Jack had objected that Webster's drama contained 'no convincing statement of the positive aspect of the doctrine of Degree', blaming the absence on Webster's 'unbalanced' mind (1949: 39–40). Lever says: 'Had Webster's mind been properly balanced – that is to say, suitably conservative – he would, Jack implies, have seen the Renaissance world as a radiant vision of God-given harmonies' (1971: 80). But Lever argues that such attempts to impose a comfortable moral coherence on the literature of the past are not only flawed, but fundamentally conservative. As he puts it in his book's introduction:

> In the present-day world, alienated in poverty and affluence, dehumanised by state bureaucracies and military machines, the most urgent study of mankind would seem to be not the eternal human condition, but the prospect of survival in the face of impersonal power drives. (1971: 1)

Thus, Lever's book focuses on the extent to which Jacobean drama explored the workings of power in its own society. His chapter on *The White Devil* and *The Duchess of Malfi*, for example, explores the resonances in the plays of the case of Lady Arbella Stuart (1971: 78–97; see 'Power and politics in Jacobean England' in Chapter 3). His analysis of *The White Devil* concentrates on the play's presentation of 'the broken humanity of Renaissance Europe' in which 'guilty and innocent alike are the victims of power' (1971: 85, 83).

The Tragedy of State inspired another major study of Jacobean drama. Jonathan Dollimore's *Radical Tragedy* was first published in 1984, and in the introduction to its second edition, Dollimore cites

Lever's book as a key influence (2010: l–liv). Dollimore expands upon Lever's analysis in a chapter devoted to *The White Devil*, exploring the play's 'demystifying of state power and ideology':

> In no other play is the identity of the individual shown to depend so much on social interaction; even as they speak protagonists are, as it were, off-centre. It is a process of displacement which shifts attention from individuals to their context and above all to a dominating power structure which constructs them as either agents or victims of power, or both. (2010: 231)

Dollimore shows that Cornelia and Isabella are both victims of ideology, sacrificing their happiness and autonomy not because they are forced to, but because they choose to out of a misguided sense of what is 'right'. Both are exploited and destroyed by the very power systems they defend. But even the characters who attempt to break away from the system in which they find themselves are doomed, too: Dollimore notes that 'Vittoria and Flamineo refuse subservience even as they serve and, in so doing, are destroyed as much by their rebellion as that which they rebel against' (2010: 246). The true victors, at the end of the play, are those who dominate its power structures. Webster's presentation of Monticelso, Dollimore argues, 'shows how state power is rendered invulnerable by identification with its 'divine' origin – how, in effect, policy gets an ideological sanction' (2010: 232).

Dollimore contextualizes his analysis by exploring some of the ideas about power and state control which were being debated during the Jacobean period. Citing Renaissance thinkers like Calvin, Machiavelli, Montaigne and Hobbes, he argues that the period's 'developing awareness of ideology in both its cognitive and material forms can best be seen by looking further at the growing concern with religion itself as an ideological practice' (2010: 11). Having analysed early modern suspicions surrounding religion and power, he does the same for law, quoting Montaigne's observation that laws were 'maintained in credit, not because they are essentially just, but because they are laws' (2010: 15). Dollimore concludes that 'the Renaissance possessed a sophisticated concept of ideology if not the word', and that 'Renaissance writers like those discussed here were actively engaged in challenging ideology' (2010: 18).

Dollimore's book has had a major influence on studies of Jacobean drama, though as Kate Aughterson notes, Dollimore 'does not really discuss the local complexities and details of Jacobean politics and philosophy, preferring a broad-sweep approach incorporating a century of different debates under one umbrella' (2001: 249). Historically minded critics since Dollimore have tended to be more specific; Dena Goldberg's *Between Worlds: A Study of the Plays of John Webster*, for example, devotes three chapters to a detailed examination of *The White Devil* in relation to Jacobean state power and law (1987: 22–77). Goldberg argues that Webster's plays are primarily concerned with the conflict between 'the desire of the individual will to express and fulfil itself' and 'the conflicting demands of the public world' (1987: 7), and that in *The White Devil* in particular,

> the orthodox arguments in favour of suppression of the individual for the sake of the community are shown to be the ideological weapons wielded by the political and religious establishment to maintain itself in power. We are made to sympathize with those individuals whose passions and aspirations force them to defy this repressive establishment. We are also made to see that their defiance can only end in their own destruction. (1987: 9)

She identifies specific criticism of 'aspects of the Jacobean legal system' (1987: 11), and goes into detail on the practicalities of Jacobean law.

Feminist criticism

A second criticism which Aughterson makes of Dollimore's book is that he omits from his analysis of the ideological debates of the Renaissance period 'a feminist critique of Jacobean patriarchy' (2001: 249) – though this is something he addresses in the introduction to his second edition. Jacobean drama has since been widely analysed by feminist critics, and *The White Devil* and *The Duchess of Malfi* have attracted a fair amount of attention – due in part, no doubt, to their presentations of female protagonists who flout the established patriarchal order.

Chapter 3 of Lisa Jardine's *Still Harping on Daughters* focuses on 'Wealth, Inheritance and the Spectre of Strong Women', and examines Vittoria, among other 'strong' heroines, by comparing their struggles with the experiences of real Elizabethan and Jacobean women, especially in relation to the law (1983: 68–102). (That chapter's discussion is heavily weighted towards *The Duchess of Malfi*.) Jardine also explores the two central female stereotypes which helped to keep women oppressed: on the one hand, the 'Madonna' figure, who like the Virgin Mary was an impossible combination of chaste, maternal and selfless, and on the other, the 'Eve' figure, who was sexual, sinful, manipulative and uncontrollable. Women who did not fulfil the patriarchal ideal of self-abnegation embodied in the former stereotype were often condemned as the latter. As Ania Loomba points out in her 1989 study *Gender, Race, Renaissance Drama*, 'the splitting of feminine identity in patriarchal stereotypes' is summed up by Bracciano in *The White Devil* when he exclaims that 'Woman to man / Is either a god or a wolf' (IV.ii.91–2; Loomba 1989: 73). Responding to Dollimore's analysis, Loomba identifies in *The White Devil* 'the combined operation of state and church and judiciary against the deviant woman' (1989: 87).

Perhaps the most sustained analysis of the play from a feminist perspective is Dympna Callaghan's *Woman and Gender in Renaissance Tragedy* (1989). Analysing *The White Devil* alongside *The Duchess of Malfi* and Shakespeare's *King Lear* and *Othello*, Callaghan's book argues that Jacobean tragedy 'places gender issues in centre stage' (1989: 1). Her analysis suggests 'that gender opposition is probably the most significant dynamic of Renaissance tragedy, and that the gender categories produced both within and outside the dramatic text are precarious and problematic' (1989: 2–3). Female protagonists like Vittoria, she argues, undermine traditional notions of women as either 'good' or 'bad', and 'her progress from transgressor to saint demolishes neat schematizations of tragic form': 'Major female characters in these plays may indeed repeat the historic transgression of Eve, but if they do, their transgression does not bring the downfall of humanity but rather...discloses the limitations of moral and social codes' (1989: 96–7). By asserting his power and demonizing Vittoria's sexuality in the trial scene, for example, Monticelso succeeds not in condemning her, but rather in exposing the inequities of both Church and patriarchy.

Assessments of the play's structure

Whereas some critics have objected to *The White Devil*'s chaotic
structure, others have gone some way to prove that it is carefully
organized. In her book *A Winter's Snake*, for example, Christina
Luckyj argues that the play is divided into two symmetrical
halves, the first ending with the trial scene. The first half, she
suggests, deals with Camillo's murder and its consequences – the
culmination of which is Vittoria's arraignment (Isabella's death
is, after all, unknown to Francisco and Monticelso until after the
trial). The second, she says, 'begins with the delayed effects of the
murder of Isabella' (1989: 109–10). Luckyj shows how the second
half mirrors the first in many ways: Bracciano's plotting dominates the first half, for example, while Francisco's dominates the
second; Flamineo plays a similar role in each half, engaging in
repeated cynical conversions first with Bracciano and then with the
disguised Francisco; Cornelia and Monticelso play similar roles in
the respective halves as the voices of morality; even the murders
of Isabella and Bracciano are similar, centred as they are around
the motifs of poison and kisses. Webster, she argues, rejected 'a
progressive, causally linked linear structure' in favour of 'repetitive
and concentric modes of organization' (1989: 151–3). She concludes
that Webster was 'a careful dramatic craftsman as well as a brilliant
poet of individual scenes and speeches', who 'was able to achieve a
"multiple unity" in his drama' (1989: 154).

Like Luckyj, Martin Wiggins identifies *The White Devil* as a play
of two halves in Chapter 9 of his 1991 study *Journeymen in Murder*.
Each half, he notes, 'has, early on, a set-piece wooing scene between
Bracciano and Vittoria, watched by Flamineo; and each ends with
violence' (1991: 169). For Wiggins, though, the characters of Flamineo
and Lodovico are the key to this patterning. Each man, he argues, 'is
the inverse of the other': 'Lodovico is a fallen aristocrat, Flamineo an
aspirant commoner; and whereas Flamineo's career spirals down-
wards to tragedy, Lodovico's takes an upward path to the consum-
mation of his revenge' (1991: 170). Flamineo begins in control,
manipulating his way towards social advancement – but by the
second half, it has become clear that such advancement is never going
to happen, and Flamineo's behaviour in the final scene is a nihilistic
recognition of this. As Wiggins points out:

At the conclusion, then, Flamineo's talk is of extinction and nothingness, whereas Lodovico has achieved fulfilment: the play presents the triumph of a man hired to be the assassin he is not, and the tragedy of an assassin without hire. (1991: 173)

Noting that Lodovico 'dominates the final moments of the play, as he did its first scene', Wiggins suggests that perhaps 'it was as Lodovico, not Flamineo as is usually supposed, that, as Webster put it, the worth of Richard Perkins's acting crowned the beginning and end of the play' (1991: 172).

Performance criticism

In his book on Webster for the *Text & Performance* series, Richard Allen Cave observes that the 'critical trend since the late fifties' has been to recognize Webster's as 'a wholly theatrical art best understood in terms of performance' (1988: 12). Cave himself makes one of the most valuable contributions to this sub-genre of Websterian criticism, devoting around half of his book to the analysis of specific twentieth-century theatrical productions. The productions of *The White Devil* which he discusses in depth are Frank Dunlop's for the National Theatre (1969) and Michael Lindsay-Hogg's for the Old Vic (1976). Cave concludes his analysis with a criticism of the 'pictorial approach' towards Webster, which relies too heavily, for him, upon costume, set and visual symbolism; a 'preferable method', he argues,

appears to allow the packed verse to make its dramatic impact within a production that is sensitive to Webster's deep preoccupation with character and his creation of a dramatic structure that, through various devices of patterning with scenes, encourages an audience to make ever subtler moral discriminations about the society his plays portray. (1988: 69)

It should be noted that Cave's conclusions rest upon firm, arguably dogmatic, understandings of what he considers to be the text's meanings: he is resistant to directors who appear to impose their own ideas upon the text. Arguably, of course, it is the job of the director to do precisely that, to a text whose meanings remain unstable and unrealized until specific staging choices are made.

A great deal of discussion of *The White Devil* in performance centres around what is perhaps the play's most self-consciously theatrical moment, the staging of the dumb-shows. Cave argues that watching Bracciano as he watches the dumb-shows 'allows us to study his mind as the deviser and director of these "shows"', and that the 'real horror of the scene' is 'his gratuitous pleasure' (1988: 35). Kate Aughterson, in another performance-centred study, discusses the dumb-shows in a chapter titled 'Webster's Theatricality'. She agrees with Cave that the scene is a 'distancing device', but notes two 'complementary but paradoxical effects':

> It displays Bracciano as shallow, cold, self-interested and voyeuristic. But it allows the audience to view the two-tiered theatrical display (the silent mime and the commenting spectators) and to look at the dumb show in a different, ethical way from Bracciano's amoral voyeurism. (2001: 164–5)

The scene, she concludes, allows Webster to demonstrate that he is 'critical of the unethical and uncommitted spectator' (2001: 181).

Both critics are influenced in this analysis by the theories of Bertolt Brecht, a German playwright and director who had an enormous influence of the theatre of the twentieth century. Brecht, a Marxist, wished to distance his audience from his plays in order 'to make the spectator adopt an attitude of inquiry and criticism' (1977: 136): the strategy, *verfremdungseffekt*, is usually translated as an 'alienation' or 'distancing' effect. A recent article by Katherine M. Carey makes the link explicit, suggesting that *The White Devil* accomplishes what Brecht advocated: the dumb-show sequences, she argues, 'break up the traditional spoken text and insert a new medium of mimed action', thereby 'serving as a very present reminder that the play is just a play' (2007: 74). Other critics, meanwhile, have used Brechtian ideas to analyse other aspects. Ralph Berry considers Webster's repeated use of rhyming *sententiae* and proverbs a 'distancing effect' in which characters 'appear to switch from living in the experience to the attempted standing outside and drawing conclusions from it'; the effect, he argues, 'is bound to be a somewhat jarring one for the audience' (1972: 29). Dollimore, meanwhile, cites Brecht directly in order to defend the 'impurity' of Jacobean drama, noting its 'elements of experiment, and "sacrilege", and its dialectic potential' (2010: 6).

As this chapter has shown, literary criticism tends to say just as much about the culture in which the criticism itself was produced as it does about its subject: Romantic critics were drawn to the 'dazzling' and 'passionate' figure of Vittoria; Victorians fretted about the play's immorality; naturalistic writers critiqued its characterization; mid-twentieth century critics who had lived through two world wars recognized its existential nihilism. Today, critics tend to resist the temptation to come to a definitive conclusion, recognizing instead that as we reread historical texts through the prisms of our own priorities and belief systems, we rediscover neglected meanings just as we reinvent new ones.

Further Reading

This is by no means an exhaustive list of works on *The White Devil* and its context, but rather an indication of where one might usefully begin further research into the play, its history and its performance. Most of these works have been cited in this book. Many of these sources are still in print, but those that are not can often be found in academic libraries, in second-hand bookshops, and online.

Editions of the text

Brennan, Elizabeth M. (ed.) (1966) *The White Devil*, New Mermaids, London: Ernest Benn. This edition has a useful, detailed introduction, and extensive notes which focus largely on linguistic and historical issues.

Brown, John Russell (ed.) (1977) *The White Devil*, The Revels Plays, Manchester: Manchester University Press. The lengthy introduction to this edition is probably one of the most influential essays on the play of the last few decades, and a wealth of material relating to Webster's sources is appended.

Brown, John Russell (ed.) (1996) *The White Devil*, Revels Student Editions, Manchester: Manchester University Press. Based on Brown's earlier version, this is a slimmer edition of the play aimed at students. Its introduction and notes are detailed and wide ranging.

Dollimore, Jonathan and Alan Sinfield (eds) (1983) *Selected Plays of John Webster*, Cambridge: Cambridge University Press. Edited by two of the leading figures of the 'cultural materialist' movement in literary criticism, this edition situates Webster's work within the political, religious and philosophical debates of the Jacobean period.

Gunby, David, David Carnegie and Antony Hammond (eds) (1995) *The Works of John Webster, Volume One: The White Devil and The Duchess of Malfi*, Cambridge: Cambridge University Press. With over 100 pages of introductory material, another 100 pages of detailed commentary, and a substantial appendix, this is the most comprehensive critical edition of the play.

This edition retains Webster's original spelling, and is thorough in its analysis of the play's historical context and its theatrical possibilities.

Luckyj, Christina (ed.) (2008) *The White Devil*, New Mermaids, 2nd edition, London: A & C Black. A particularly useful text for the theatre practitioner or the drama student, this edition analyses modern productions of the play in its introduction, and includes detailed notes on staging throughout.

Trussler, Simon (ed.) (1996) *The White Devil*, Drama Classics, London: Nick Hern. Based on Brown's edition of the text but without his detailed notes, this is probably the smallest and least expensive edition of the play currently in print. It has a short but useful introduction.

Weis, René (ed.) (1996) *The Duchess of Malfi and Other Plays*, Oxford World's Classics, Oxford: Oxford University Press. A short introduction analyses the play alongside *The Duchess of Malfi* and two of Webster's later plays, *The Devil's Law-Case* and *A Cure for a Cuckold*, all of which are included in this collection. Explanatory notes are compiled at the end of the book rather than on the page with Webster's text.

Plays by Webster and his contemporaries

Most of these texts are available in multiple editions; those that are not can usually be downloaded for free from the Internet Archive (www.archive.org) or, at subscribing institutions, from Early English Books Online (eebo.chadwyck.com). Those marked with an asterisk are contained in Bevington, David (ed.) (2002) *English Renaissance Drama: A Norton Anthology*, New York: W. W. Norton & Company.

*Anon. (attributed to Thomas Middleton) (1607) *The Revenger's Tragedy*. A violent and cynical revenge tragedy of the period, this has much in common with Webster's play.

Anon. (1620) *Swetnam the Woman-Hater*. Also performed at the Red Bull, this play stages an inversion of Vittoria's trial, in which a misogynistic man is arraigned by women.

Dekker, Thomas and John Webster (1604) *Westward Ho!* and (1605) *Northward Ho!* These city comedies, while very different from *The White Devil*, contain farcical elements which resurface in Webster's later play.

Dekker, Thomas and John Webster (1607) *The Famous History of Sir Thomas Wyatt*. Like *The White Devil*, this play tells the story of a woman caught up in a struggle for political power.

*Ford, John (1633) *'Tis Pity She's A Whore*. A later revenge tragedy about an incestuous affair between a brother and sister, this has much in common with Webster's play, and shows his influence.

*Kyd, Thomas (c. 1587) *The Spanish Tragedy*. A hugely popular and influential revenge tragedy, this is essential reading for a study of the genre.

*Marlowe, Christopher (c. 1589) *The Jew of Malta*. This play features a Machiavellian anti-hero, and, in its prologue, a highly fictionalized portrait of Machiavelli himself.

*Marston, John (1604) *The Malcontent*. Webster wrote the 'Induction' for this play, and it was clearly an influence on the creation of his own 'malcontents'.

Shakespeare, William (c. 1600) *Hamlet*. The most famous revenge tragedy of them all, *Hamlet* shares some key features with *The White Devil* (a ghost, feigned and real madness, a malcontent), and is quoted directly in it.

Shakespeare, William (1606) *King Lear*. A tragedy about power, politics and deception, this also has much in common with Webster's play. Again, Webster borrows some key lines.

*Webster, John (1614) *The Duchess of Malfi*. Essential reading for any student of *The White Devil*; most criticism on the play deals with both tragedies.

Webster, John (1619) *The Devil's Law-Case*. A later play in which Webster extended the tragicomic formula he had begun to explore in *The White Devil*. As its title suggests, it is concerned with the complexities of the law, and like *The White Devil*, it hinges on a climactic trial scene.

Sources and contexts

These sources are discussed in Chapters 1 and 3. Out-of-copyright texts are generally available online.

Adams, Thomas (1612) 'The White Devil, or, The Hypocrite Uncased' in Joseph Angus (ed.) (1861), *The Works of Thomas Adams*, Edinburgh: James Nichol, vol ii, pp. 221–53.

Anon. (1620) 'Hic Mulier: Or the Man-Woman' in David Damrosch, Constance Jordan and Clare Carroll (eds) (2006) *The Longman Anthology of British Literature, Volume 1B: The Early Modern Period* (3rd edition), Harlow: Longman, pp. 1527–30.

Bacon, Francis (1972) *Essays*, London: Dent.

Briggs, Julia (1997) *This Stage-Play World: Texts and Contexts, 1580–1625*, Oxford: Oxford University Press.

Gurr, Andrew (1992) *The Shakespearean Stage 1574–1642*, Cambridge: Cambridge University Press.

Gurr, Andrew (2004) *Playgoing in Shakespeare's London*, (3rd edition), Cambridge: Cambridge University Press.

Jardine, Lisa (1996) *Reading Shakespeare Historically*, London: Routledge.

Lindley, David (1993) *The Trials of Frances Howard: Fact and Fiction at the Court of King James*, London: Routledge.

Marriott, W. K. (ed. and trans.) (1908) *The Prince by Nicolo Machiavelli*, London: J. M. Dent.

Swetnam, Joseph (1615) 'The Arraignment of Lewd, Idle, Froward, and Unconstant Women' in David Damrosch, Constance Jordan and Clare Carroll (eds) (2006) *The Longman Anthology of British Literature, Volume 1B: The Early Modern Period* (3rd edition), Harlow: Longman, pp. 1514–17.

Von Klarwill, Victor (ed.) (1926) *The Fugger News-Letters*, second series, trans. Pauline de Chary, London: G. P. Putnam's sons.

Anthologies of criticism

The following texts compile a wide variety of critical writings on Webster's plays, in most cases stretching back to the seventeenth century. With the most recent of them having been published in 1984, though, none of them include examples of the most up-to-date criticism.

Holdsworth, R. V. (ed.) (1984) *Webster: The White Devil and The Duchess of Malfi: A Casebook*, Basingstoke: Palgrave Macmillan.

Hunter, G. K. and S. K. (eds) (1969) *John Webster: A Critical Anthology*, London: Penguin.

Moore, Don D. (ed.) (1981) *John Webster: The Critical Heritage*, London: Routledge.

Morris, Brian (ed.) (1970) *John Webster: A Mermaid Critical Commentary*, London: Ernest Benn.

Criticism pre-1950

Most of these sources are discussed in Chapter 5, and many are available to download from the Internet Archive (www.archive.org).

Archer, William (1893) 'Webster, Lamb, and Swinburne', *New Review*, reprinted in Holdsworth 1984: 45–8.

Bradbrook, M. C. (1935) (repr. 1960) *Themes and Conventions of Elizabethan Tragedy*, Cambridge: Cambridge University Press.

Bradley, A. C. (1904) *Shakespeare Tragedy: Lectures on Hamlet, Othello, King Lear, Macbeth*, London: Macmillan.

Brooke, Rupert (1916) *John Webster and the Elizabethan Drama*, London: Sidgwick & Jackson.

Cecil, David (1949) *Poets and Story-Tellers*, London: Constable.

Eliot, T. S. (1932) *Essays on Elizabethan Drama*, New York: Harcourt, Brace & Company.

Eliot, T. S. (1950) *Selected Essays*, New York: Harcourt, Brace & Company.

Hazlitt, William (1820) (repr. 1890) *Lectures on the Literature of the Age of Elizabeth*, London: George Bell & Sons.

'H.M.' (1818) 'Analytical Essays on the Early English Dramatists', *Blackwood's Edinburgh Magazine*, reprinted in Holdsworth 1984: 34–7.

Jack, Ian (1949) 'The Case of John Webster', *Scrutiny* 16, 38–43.

Kingsley, Charles (1856) (repr. 1885) 'Plays and Puritans' in *Plays and Puritans, and Other Historical Essays*, London: Macmillan, pp. 1–79.

Knights, L. C. (1933) 'How Many Children Had Lady Macbeth? An Essay in the Theory and Practice of Shakespeare Criticism' in *Explorations: Essays in Criticism*, New York: George W. Stewart, 1947, pp. 15–54.

Lamb, Charles (1808) (repr. 1845) *Specimens of English Dramatic Poets Who Lived About the Time of Shakespeare*, New York: Wiley & Putnam.

Lucas, F. L. (1927) (repr. 1967) 'General Introduction' to *The Complete Works of John Webster*, London: Chatto & Windus.

Poel, William (1893) 'A New Criticism of Webster's *Duchess of Malfi*', *Library Review* 2, 21–4.

Shaw, George Bernard (1932) *Our Theatre in the Nineties*, London: Constable.

Smith, James (1939) 'The Tragedy of Blood', *Scrutiny* 8, 265–80.

Swinburne, Algernon Charles (1886) (repr. 1908) *The Age of Shakespeare*, London: Chatto & Windus.

Watson, William (1893) *Excursions in Criticism*, London: Elkin Mathews & John Lane.

Wendell, Barrett (1904) *The Temper of the Seventeenth Century in England*, New York: Charles Scribner's Sons.

Criticism post-1950

Like the texts in the previous category, most of these sources are discussed in Chapter 5. Most are still in print, and should be stocked in academic libraries.

Aughterson, Kate (2001) *Webster: The Tragedies*, Basingstoke: Palgrave Macmillan.

Berry, Ralph (1972) *The Art of John Webster*, Oxford: Clarendon Press.

Bogard, Travis (1955) *The Tragic Satire of John Webster*, Berkeley: University of California Press.

Boklund, Gunnar (1966) *The Sources of 'The White Devil'*, New York: Haskell House.

Bradbrook, M. C. (1980) *John Webster, Citizen and Dramatist*, London: Weidenfeld & Nicolson.

Brecht, Bertolt (1977) *Brecht on Theatre*, trans. J. Willett, London: Eyre Methuen.

Bromley, Laura G. (1991) 'The Rhetoric of Feminine Identity in *The White Devil*' in Dorothea Kehler and Susan Baker (eds) *In Another Country: Feminist Perspectives on Renaissance Drama*, Metchuen, NJ: Scarecrow, pp. 50–70.

Brown, John Russell (1977) 'Introduction', *The White Devil*, The Revels Plays, Manchester: Manchester University Press.

Callaghan, Dympna (1989) *Woman and Gender in Renaissance Tragedy*, Hemel Hempstead: Harvester Wheatsheaf.

Carey, Katherine M. (2007) 'The Aesthetics of Immediacy and Hypermediation: The Dumb Shows in Webster's *The White Devil*', *New Theatre Quarterly* 23: 1, 73–80.

Dent, R. W. (1960) *John Webster's Borrowing*, Berkeley: University of California Press.

Dollimore, Jonathan (2010) *Radical Tragedy: Religion, Ideology and Power in the Drama of Shakespeare and his Contemporaries*, reissued 3rd edition, Basingstoke: Palgrave Macmillan.

Forker, Charles R. (1986) *The Skull Beneath the Skin: The Achievement of John Webster*, Carbondale: Southern Illinois University Press.

Gill, Roma (1966) ' "Quaintly Done": A Reading of *The White Devil*', *Essays and Studies* 19, 41–59.

Goldberg, Dena (1987) *Between Worlds: A Study of the Plays of John Webster*, Waterloo: Wilfrid Laurier University Press.

Jardine, Lisa (1983) *Still Harping on Daughters: Women and Drama in the Age of Shakespeare*, Brighton: Harvester Press.

Lever, J. W. (1971) *The Tragedy of State: A Study of Jacobean Drama*, London: Methuen.

Loomba, Ania (1989) *Gender, Race, Renaissance Drama*, Manchester: Manchester University Press.

Luckyj, Christina (1989) *A Winter's Snake: Dramatic Form in the Tragedies of John Webster*, Athens, GA: The University of Georgia Press.

Pearson, Jacqueline (1980) *Tragedy and Tragicomedy in the Plays of John Webster*, Manchester: Manchester University Press.

Ribner, Irving (1962) *Jacobean Tragedy: The Quest for Moral Order*, New York: Barnes & Noble.

Wiggins, Martin (1991) *Journeymen in Murder: The Assassin in English Renaissance Drama*, Oxford: Clarendon.

Wiggins, Martin (1997) 'Conjuring the Ghosts of *The White Devil*', *The Review of English Studies*, 48: 192, 448–70.

On modern performances of the play

By far the largest amount of material on specific modern productions of *The White Devil* is to be found in newspaper and magazine reviews; these are widely available online and elsewhere, so I have not listed any here. The following sources are pieces of academic writing which examine one or more of the productions discussed in Chapter 4 at some length.

Band, Tom (2009) 'Review of John Webster's *The White Devil* (directed by Jonathan Munby) at the Menier Chocolate Factory', *Shakespeare* 5, 98–100.

Carnegie, David (1995) 'Theatrical introduction' to *The White Devil* in David Gunby, David Carnegie and Antony Hammond (eds) *The Works of John Webster, Volume One*, Cambridge: Cambridge University Press, pp. 84–120. This gives an overview of a variety of twentieth-century productions in Britain, America and Australia.

Cave, Richard Allen (1988) *Text & Performance: The White Devil and The Duchess of Malfi*, Basingstoke: Palgrave Macmillan. Part two focuses on Frank Dunlop and Michael Lindsay-Hogg's productions.

Jones, Emrys (1991) 'Too Roomy for Intimacies', *Times Literary Supplement*, 28 June. This is an academic review of Philip Prowse's production.

Moore, Don D. (1965) 'John Webster in the Modern Theatre', *Educational Theatre Journal* 17: 4, 314–21. This article gives an overview of a variety of twentieth century productions up to the mid-1960s.

Schafer, Elizabeth (1997) '*The White Devil*: Royal Shakespeare Company', *Research Opportunities in Renaissance Drama* 36, 117–19.

Smith, P. J. (2001) '*The White Devil*, directed by Philip Franks', *Cahiers Élisabéthains* 59, 98–100.

Tippler, Nick (2000) 'Cunning with Pistols: Observations on Gale Edwards's 1996–7 RSC production of John Webster's *The White Devil*' in E. J. Esche (ed.) *Shakespeare and his Contemporaries in Performance*, Aldershot: Ashgate, pp. 275–88.

Index